BRIGHT IDEAS

Computer A

CW01668106

Written by Juliet J
Steve Hartland and John Tol

Published by Scholastic Publications Ltd,
Villiers House, Clarendon Avenue,
Leamington Spa, Warwickshire CV32 5PR

Written by Juliet Joy, John Tolley and
Steven Hartland
Edited by Janet Fisher
Sub-edited by Magdalena Hernas
Illustrations by Lesley Smith
Front and back covers designed by
Anna Oliwa
Photograph by Martyn Chillmaid
Artwork by Steve Williams Design,
Leicester

Printed in Great Britain by Loxley Brothers
Ltd, Sheffield

British Library Cataloguing in Publication Data
A catalogue record for this book is
available from the British Library.

ISBN 0 590 53045 3

Contents

Introduction

WHY INFORMATION TECHNOLOGY?

Information Technology (IT) now has its place within the national curriculums of the United Kingdom and we have to ensure that, as such, it is evident both within our curriculum planning and classroom activities. There are, of course, many other reasons for teaching IT which stem from both life outside school and also from experience gained from classrooms over the past few years. Now that IT has its own attainment target, it is tempting to think of it as a discrete subject. This, however, would be a mistake as IT is a cross-curricular tool which should be a teaching aid in all the areas of the curriculum.

It is worth emphasising here that information and computer technology are not synonymous. Computers are an increasingly influential and pervasive form of information technology but they are not the only form. Basically, IT is concerned with any form of technology which can be used to enhance communication. Obviously, machines such as videos, audio cassettes and television sets could also satisfy this definition. In the classroom, the computer may prove to be the major vehicle for the delivery of IT but it will not necessarily be the only one.

Today's world is permeated at all levels with examples of computer technology, some so mundane that we may hardly notice them. Children are growing up in an environment where money appears from cash dispensers in the wall in response to a few key presses on a number pad, where their favourite television programme can be recorded automatically while they are out shopping with their parents or where they wake up to a warm house because the heating has switched itself on while they were still slumbering. The world of work is

profoundly affected by IT. Most offices are equipped with computers, fax machines and photocopiers. Factories use computer technology to control stock, to help design products and to perform routine production tasks. Furthermore, the pace and acceleration of change will mean that the influence of IT will become deeper and more widespread. Clearly, it is our duty to help children to understand all these processes so that they can become active participants in an increasingly technological society.

Computers have been introduced into classrooms over the past decade and their use has been steadily increasing over the last five years. What beneficial aspects have been noticed during that time?

- Many teachers have noted that computers have proved highly motivational. They can stimulate children to produce both a high quality and quantity of work.
- Computers are good presentational tools. A print-out looks professional and work can be edited easily, without the need to start again.
- Information Technology need not be a singular activity; it often succeeds best in group situations. A computer screen can be made into a very public place where ideas are pooled and discussed. The computer can prove the perfect forum and stimulus for group discussion and co-operation. For example, a group of children can devise and produce a story or they can develop a musical composition.
- Very often, teachers want children to explore real-life situations but need to stay within the physical confines of the classroom. Information Technology can provide one vehicle by which the real world can be simulated. Many programs exist which allow children to follow an 'adventure' where they need to solve problems to reach a successful conclusion. Other programs attempt to simulate real life more closely and put the user in the place of, for example, the urban fox trying to survive, or the diver exploring an old wreck, or the environmentalist searching for evidence for an inquiry. These types of program can become the central stimulus from which all sorts of cross-curricular work can develop (most of it, probably, away from the computer itself).
- For many children, the computer offers not just the opportunity to enrich and extend the curriculum but, more crucially, a method of access. The extent and variety of IT use within special needs is too great to discuss fully here but it may be useful to consider two examples to illustrate its possibilities. Firstly, a child experiencing difficulty producing written work may be helped by the use of a concept keyboard with overlays which contain keywords for a particular topic. Secondly, a blind child may be able to produce written work fluently in Braille which a mainstream teacher cannot understand. With information technology, it is possible to produce simultaneously both Braille copy and ordinary text 'translation' on a linked printer, thus allowing the teacher to read the child's work without needing to understand the Braille system.

THE FIVE STRANDS OF IT

The National Curriculum documents split IT into five strands: Communicating Information, Handling Information, Modelling and Simulation, Measurement and Control and Applications and Effects.

- Communicating Information

This area covers not only text but sounds and pictures as well. Therefore, work with music and art packages will prove just as relevant as work with a word processor or a Desk-Top Publisher (DTP).

- Handling Information

Computers are very good at storing large amounts of data and allowing the user to sift through that information and find answers to questions. Children need to work with databases at a simple level so that they can begin to understand how the larger, more sophisticated databases in the outside world function.

- Modelling and Simulation

Children can begin to work in this field with the help of an adventure program that may set them various problems to which they have to find solutions to make progress. Some programs attempt to simulate real life quite accurately: you may be confronted with the problems facing a racing driver and his back-up team or you could become the urban fox trying to survive in a hostile environment.

- Measurement and Control

You can connect your computer to various devices which you can use to measure changes in the environment: for example, you could use a temperature sensor to record the variations in temperature in a room over a period of time. It is also possible to control the movement of various robots, the most common of which is probably the floor turtle.

- Applications and Effects

It is important that children begin to study how computers are used in the world outside school and begin to understand the influence computer technology has on the world outside the classroom.

The 'bright ideas' in this book are intended to help you to develop pupils' abilities within these 'strands' and will usually refer you to the area of IT they are intended to support.

CHOICE OF SOFTWARE

There is a mass of software available today and the best tactic is probably to seek advice before buying. Your local LEA computer centre is likely to be your best source of free advice from people who will probably have used the programs actually running in the classroom. When buying a computer system it is important to check what relevant software is available. It is not much use having a technically brilliant machine if there is no software available to support the work in your classroom.

Software can be divided into two categories: structured software and content-free or framework software. Structured software comes ready to use; the content of the program cannot be radically changed by the user. These types of program prove easy to start up and run and there are many examples of well-written 'structured' programs. The major drawback with relying on this type of software is that you will need to keep a large software library to meet all your curriculum needs. Obviously, there may be a program which suits one particular curriculum area, but what do you do if there really is nothing suitable for another topic? Buying individual programs

to suit every niche of your curriculum will prove not only expensive but very difficult to match to every curriculum requirement.

Content-free software may provide a partial answer to this problem. Major types of content-free software include word processors, databases and programming packages such as LOGO. No matter what the curriculum area, it will be possible to create writing based around it using a word-processing package or to collect and examine evidence using a database. This type of software often allows you to make your own resources to match your classroom requirements. With a concept keyboard program, for example, you could make your own overlays to support work on a particular historical period. These programs are flexible and powerful. You do not need to own a large library of programs because you can adapt them to suit many varied topics and levels of ability. Content-free programs often initially require more effort on the part of the user but, once mastered, will allow teachers to tailor computer resources much more closely to classroom requirements.

The best solution to the problem of starting and maintaining a library of programs is probably to use a mixture of the two types of software. Indeed, once you are familiar with various content-free packages, purchasing examples of structured software becomes easier – you only need to buy a program to support a particular topic if it really is of the required quality (and, if there is nothing suitable, you may well be able to produce some resources of your own!).

CLASSROOM MANAGEMENT

One issue constantly confronting the classroom teachers is the problem of managing the microcomputer within their classroom. Each chapter in the book has a section which advises on how best to organise particular computer activities, but it is important to make some general points here.

One problem that teachers continually raise is that of keyboard time – this is particularly crucial where classes have to share a computer. Even if you have a computer permanently in your classroom, activities such as word processing can be difficult to cater for. If you are sharing a computer, perhaps one answer is to change the policy of having the computer timetabled between classes (class 1 Monday, class 2 Tuesday and so on). It may be better to allow a class to have sole use of the computer for half a term, and then another class the next half term. Each class would be able to use the computer intensively for a period of time, but then would have to 'do without' any computer access for a similar period. This approach would obviously have implications for planning, especially in the case of class topics; you may have a machine for one topic but not another.

IT work will run most smoothly in your classroom if you integrate computer work into your general classroom work. It should not be an extra which is 'bolted on' to other curricular activities. Most of the activities described in this book are cross-curricular in nature and will work best if they form a valid part of the whole learning experience.

One last point about classroom management – it is vitally important that all children are given equal access to the computer and especially that girls and boys are given equal opportunity to work at the keyboard.

ABOUT THIS BOOK

The chapters that follow all use particular elements of computer work as their focus; there is one chapter on word processing, another on databases and so on. None of the chapters is intended to be a comprehensive introduction to work in that particular field, but rather to provide a collection of practical classroom ideas that will help either to initiate or extend your classroom work with the computer in a particular area. All the sections give advice on what is required to implement an activity, implications for classroom management and guidelines on how to carry out and develop these activities with your children.

Word processing

This chapter deals with the basic word processor and its functions. Many word processors have enhancements which allow great variety in how written work is presented, but the greatest value of the word processor is how it prepares text. Although there may be a good reason for typing out a piece of hard writing, a child is simply using the word processor as a presentation tool. The most important functions of a word processor should enable a child to:

- convey ideas to the screen where they can be read clearly;
- edit the text to correct spelling and punctuation;
- insert and delete words and phrases to enhance the text;
- move pieces of the text to another part of the work;
- save and retrieve the text so that it can be used over a period of time;
- print the material on a printer.

The use of the printer usually appears to be a form of presentation but its use in this chapter allows some work to be done away from the computer, giving more children access to this scarce resource. The printed material, or hard copy, can be studied for mistakes, discussed with other members of the class and, if copies are made, can become the focus for a particular teaching point. Many children find it easier to edit and enhance their work when it is on paper rather than on the screen. It is also important for some children that the word processor can be used in conjunction with a concept keyboard. A spelling checker will also help with the correction of text.

Technology in the National Curriculum places the functions of a word processor at different levels in the Attainment Targets and it is important that the word processor has the facilities needed when children are working at these levels. For example, at Level 4 in the strand concerned with communicating information, children must be able to use information technology to retrieve, develop, organise and present work. A simple word processor without a facility to move blocks of text could not deliver the 'organise' part of the statement without the work having to be rewritten.

It is also necessary for children working at any particular level to give them activities that will cause them to use the facilities available. The following activities are concerned with using the facilities offered by the word processor, not just in learning how to use them, but in giving children access to an activity which would be difficult or onerous if written by hand. Ensure that all children have access to the computer by keeping activities short but valuable.

What's for dinner?

Age range
Five to seven.

Group size
Pairs.

What you need
A word processor or a computer with a word-processing facility, a printer, sample restaurant menus.

Starting points
Ask the children what they like best for dinner. Talk about school dinners and what is served. Have the children been to a restaurant? How do they know what to choose? Show them some sample menus and discuss how the menus are split up into parts. Suggest the children make a menu for school dinners.

What to do
Type a menu into the word processor with the word MENU at the top and the day of the week underneath. (A more sophisticated menu could be produced if the software is available.) Depending on the age and ability of the children, split up the menu under headings such as MAIN COURSES and SWEETS or PUDDINGS. The various courses could be a series of choices.

Set up a contact at school for the children to ask each morning about what is on the menu for that day. Whether the contact is the cook or someone else, ensure that their response fits the ability of the children. A written response would need to be read easily.

Show the children how to delete the appropriate parts of the menu, such as the day, and insert new material. Each day, select a pair of children to go to their information source and ask what is on the menu for that day. Then ask them to load the old menu from disk, alter the day and the food items, print a copy of the menu and save the new menu to disk.

This fairly simple task includes many of the keyboard and word-processing skills needed for basic word processing. Carrying out the task over a period of time will establish these skills.

Follow-up
Ask the children to make a 'good for you' and 'not good for you' list of foods and/or a shopping list of items the cook would need to produce the food on the menu.

A real mix-up

Age range
Seven to eleven.

Group size
Pairs or small groups.

What you need
A word processor or a computer with a word-processing facility, small cards, a pencil.

Starting points
Children do not always listen very well to instructions and consequently make mistakes. Take time to talk to children about the importance of giving instructions correctly and what happens when things to wrong. Give them examples to examine such as giving directions, building a model or operating a computer program. Encourage children to give instructions for a simple task, for example, eating a biscuit or putting on a shoe.

What to do
Make a set of cards with simple tasks appropriate to the children's age and ability. These could be based on directions ranging from how to get to the headteacher's office to how to get home. Alternatively, they could be instructions on how to obtain BBC 2 on the television or how to record a programme on a video. Humorous or serious, they are all valid. Write on each card, 'Give instructions on how to . . .' and then write the task such as 'Sharpen a pencil'.

Give each group a card according to their ability and allow them to put their instructions into the computer. Tell them to make each instruction short and to begin each on a new line. Make sure the children know how to insert an instruction if they have missed one out.

After taking opportunities to carry out the instructions with the children, allow them to revise them if necessary. Complete the activity by asking the children to mix up the order of their instructions. (You may have to show them how to 'cut and paste'.) These new versions can be saved using a different file name. Give the cards and the names of the mixed up-file to different groups and ask them to rearrange the instructions. Give more able children only the name of the file so that they do not know which activity the instructions are for.

Follow-up
Allow children to make up instruction sheets that have a function in the classroom, for example, instructions for playing games, loading a computer program and operating a tape recorder. They may not always be able to construct the sheets on the computer but they could type in a final working version. Copies of instructions can be printed out as others become worn. Those that do not work well can be enhanced.

An exciting day, I think!

Age range
Eight to eleven.

Group size
Three or the whole class.

What you need
A word processor or a computer with a word processing facility, notes or memory of a large amount of information, such as an outing to an educational establishment, a visit of an interesting person or an educational television programme, a printer.

Starting points
Children often need to recall a large amount of information and record it in some way. Each child will have some recollection but only an exceptional child will remember most of what she has seen or heard. Ask a child to tell the rest of the class what happened during the activity (the school visit or programme) and ask others to add to the account. Finish when it becomes obvious that no one child can recount everything.

What to do
Explain to the children that the process of searching for memories or new ideas is called brainstorming and that if someone writes them all down, they are more likely to end up with an accurate account. Invite the children to brainstorm a chosen topic. Do this with the whole class and ask a quick typist to put the information into the word processor. Alternatively, put the children into groups and let them enter the pieces of information that they recall. Encourage the children to keep their information very brief. Ask some groups to put the information into chronological order and let others check the spelling. Give printed copies of the final collection of information to each child or group and ask the children to make a final expanded version by hand or on the computer.

All children can contribute to this brainstorming and the hard copy of the information will allow less able children to increase their use of vocabulary when writing the final draft.

Follow-up

Use the computer for brainstorming until children initiate it themselves. A simplified example of this is the production of a word list to help with a piece of writing. For instance, the children could suggest as many words as possible for an autumn poem.

Words cost money

Age range

Nine to ten.

Group size

Pairs or small groups.

What you need

A word processor or a computer with a word-processing facility, a collection of 'for sale' advertisements from a local newspaper (examples of charges for advertising space would also be useful), pictures, brochures or catalogues of bicycles.

Starting points

Children will be used to writing for different audiences and it is likely that they have sometimes been restricted by the amount they have been able to write. However, they are unlikely to have had to limit their writing because of cost. This activity deals with the conflict between information required and the cost of providing the information. Start by talking about the problems of insufficient information and set the example of trying to buy a bicycle.

What to do

Ask the children to think about the sort of bicycle they would like to own or already have. Give them the pictures and catalogues and ask them to imagine that someone has a bicycle for sale. Encourage them to write down all the questions they would like to ask about it before considering buying it. Put the list on the computer and print it out if time allows.

Explain to the children that they should now pretend to have a bicycle to sell and that they must put an advertisement in a newspaper. Point out that there will be a lot of advertisements in the paper and there may only be one buyer so they have to attract the reader's attention. The price should not come into it as everyone must advertise their bicycle at the same price of £100.

When all the groups have put their advertisement into the computer, introduce the cost factor. Explain that each word will cost £1, so if they have used a lot of words they may not have any money left after the sale of the bicycle. Let the children attempt to shorten their work as much as possible, using real advertisements for guidance.

Follow-up

Bring the children together and let them evaluate each other's work. Ask them to identify other times when we need to use as few words as possible. Emergency phone calls and telemessages are such examples.

Daily diary

Age range

Six to eight.

Group size

Pairs or small groups.

What you need

A word processor or a computer with a word-processing facility, seeds or bulbs, plant pots or jam-jars, compost, blotting paper, water.

Starting points

Ask the children if they have good memories. Encourage a child who says yes to try to remember what they did in class the week before. Discuss why and when it is important to be accurate. One such example is when

giving travel directions. Discuss with the children what they could do to help them remember, leading the children to the idea of a diary. Use the discussion to talk about plants. What happens when they grow? What happens first? How long does it take?

What to do

With the children's help, plant seeds or bulbs in plant pots or jam jars, according to the instructions. Beans or peas fastened with blotting paper to the side of a jam-jar containing water will allow the children to observe the growth clearly.

Ask each group of children to set up a file on the word processor for storing data about the growth of the plant. Each day let the children load the file into the word processor, put the day and date and explain what is happening to the plant. They can then save the file ready for the next day. The information that they enter can be partially determined beforehand. This could be the height of the plant, the length of the root and the number of leaves. Let the children expand the list when they make other observations. Encourage the children to compare the facts with the previous day and add any comments, such as 'new roots have started growing on the old one'.

Ask the children to read through the old entries and identify important events. If nothing has happened for several days, ask them to combine them into one entry. When you feel that the children have enough entries, let them print them out and use the copies to analyse how the plant grew. Encourage them to answer questions such as 'Which comes first, the root or the stem?'

If a concept keyboard is available, let the children use it to enter some items such as the date and some of the measurement statements, for example, 'The height of the plant to day is'. This makes the entries much quicker to input.

Let the children save the file each day with a different name. If the first day is called PLANT1 and this is saved on a Monday, then each subsequent file is saved as PLANT followed by the number of the day. This means that if a file is lost for any reason you will always have the previous day's file to use.

Follow-up

Let children keep other diaries including those based on personal events such as reading books, watching television or family celebrations.

Whose is it and what is it?

Age range

Six to eleven.

Group size

Individuals.

What you need

A word processor or a computer with a word-processing facility, a printer, scissors, adhesive.

Starting points

This basic activity can be done with children of any age. If the children have previously used the computer for labelling, they should progress to using presentation packages where the labels can be enhanced with borders and other graphical touches. In this activity the decoration of the labels will depend on centring, spacing and tabs. Where the word processor has a choice of fonts, discuss with the children which ones are most suitable to use.

Look at the way children put their names on artwork or other belongings. Ask them to suggest ways that would improve the problem of not knowing what it is and who has produced it.

What to do

Encourage the children to look for areas where simple labels or notices could be improved by using the computer. Names and titles on work folders or labels on cupboards or storage spaces are ideal for this type of work.

Set up the computer attached to a printer with

continuous-feed paper. Show the children how to create a simple label for the painting, drawing or model they have worked on. For example:

Encourage the children to make a similar label on the computer. Let them print it out, cut off the paper, trim it and stick it on their work.

Follow-up

Ask the children to identify some objects which might need a label, which they could then design and produce individually.

The secret message

Age range

Nine to eleven.

Group size

Pairs or small groups.

What you need

A word processor or a computer with a word-processing facility, a copy of the alphabet, some examples of codes.

Starting points

This activity uses the search and replace facility of the word processor to enable children to produce a coded message which other children can attempt to decode.

Without this facility, the task of trying out different ideas could become onerous.

Discuss with the children the idea of codes and why they are used. Not all codes are used for secrecy, for instance the Dewey book classification system and bar codes in supermarkets.

What to do

Ask the children to write down something that they want to remain secret. It must be no longer than a sentence. Then, using the alphabet, ask them to find as many letters as they can which are not used in the sentence. These can then be used to replace letters in their secret sentence. If the child runs out of letters to replace others, let him use the replaced ones.

Ask the children to enter the sentence into the computer and use the search and replace facility to replace letters that have not been used. For example, if the letter Z does not appear in the sentence, the children must ask the computer to replace all As with the letter Z. This can be done as many times as required.

Let the children begin with very simple examples such as replacing the vowels or limiting replacement to a small number of letters.

Ask other groups of children to try to solve the code by looking for clues and replacing the coded letters with the correct ones.

Follow-up

Embark on a topic on codes which will involve a great deal of problem solving. Let the children find other ways of using the computer to construct secret messages such as replacing As with Z and Bs with Y and so on. Can they replace letters with their number in the alphabet to create a message in secret code?

The picture tells a story

Age range

Nine to eleven.

Group size

Pairs or small groups.

What you need

A word processor or a computer with a word-processing facility, pictures of people from magazines or books. (The people should be known to you, though not necessarily to the children and preferably they should be involved in an activity and dressed in a variety of ways.)

Starting points

Describing someone is usually quite difficult for children. Using a word processor will enable the children to order their observations. Tell the children a story of an imaginary crime. Show the children two or three pictures of people and explain that these people were seen at the scene of the crime. How would they describe them to the police? Which one do they think committed the crime and why? After some discussion, identify the three people, making sure that the villain is the most innocent-looking person.

What to do

Take a selection of pictures not used previously, give one to each group and ask them to describe the person as if they were talking to the police. Let one child take the 'statement' and input the description on the word processor. Then ask them to make up the person's background. Who is he? Where does he live? Does he have a family? Does he have a job and, if so, what is it? Is he a 'nice' person? Why? Where was he when you saw him? Where was he going? What sort of expression was on his face? Why?

To add further interest, put a time limit on the activity or the real criminal might escape.

Follow-up

Looking through the children's work, an obvious villain may emerge. If the characters are people whom you know personally, it will be fun to compare the children's ideas with the reality of the situation, particularly if a nasty character turns out to be the local vicar. Use the children's work in inventing some more crimes or incidents and asking the children to decide whether or not it is their character and why.

Five-minute drama

Age range

Eight to eleven.

Group size

Small groups.

What you need

A word processor or a computer with a word-processing facility, a selection of characters for five-minute plays (these can be people, animals or objects depending on the age and ability of the children).

Starting points

Start with a joke. 'What did the . . . say to the . . .? Discuss with the children the idea of animals or objects talking. How could they write down a conversation? Show the children how a play is written.

What to do

Ask the children to take two characters. Older children could have three or four characters. Ask them to imagine that the characters meet or something happens to cause them to speak to one another. Invite them to write a play about their meeting. Let them consider whether it is friendly, unfriendly, funny, frightening or sad. Ask them to write directly on to the computer, trying out sections and editing where necessary.

Follow-up

Encourage the children to make insertions and deletions to the play and to put in some extra material such as action and stage directions. Let the children perform their work to an audience.

Latest report

Age range

Seven to eleven.

Group size

Individuals or small groups.

What you need

A word processor or a computer with a word-processing facility (if you have a desk-top publishing package or a program that allows you to produce a newspaper, use this instead), a printer, A3 paper, scissors, adhesive, pencils, felt-tipped pens.

Starting points

Discuss the production of newspapers and what they contain. Where does the news come from? Is it possible to produce a class newspaper? Do you have enough news? Who are you writing for?

What to do

Ask the children to make a list of types of articles in a newspaper. Using the computer, invite them to be reporters of sports events, films, television programmes and so on and to write reports of these events. Let them use a folder or noticeboard to store printed copies of their reports.

When there appears to be enough material, let them begin producing a newspaper. If you only have a simple word processor, restrict the line length to a half or a quarter of the width of an A4 sheet of paper. When printed out, this will be the width of each column and the children can stick them on to an A3 sheet of paper.

Encourage the children to produce pictures by hand or by using a camera or computer. They can then stick these on to the paper alongside the reports.

Follow-up

- Let the children explore different ways of producing the hard copy. This will depend on the sophistication of your computer software.
- Ask the children to base subsequent newspapers on a history topic or on an imaginary place with different landscapes and people.

Does it rhyme?

Age range

Seven to ten.

Group size

Pairs or small groups.

What you need

A word processor or a computer with a word-processing facility.

Starting points

Following a poetry reading, a story or a period of visual stimulation, discuss with the children what makes a good poem.

What to do

Take a theme such as snakes and encourage the children to produce as many words as possible which sound like snakes or would be useful when talking about them. Let the children enter these straight into the computer and save as a file.

Ask each group of children to load the file and use the words to construct a poem on the computer. The computer will enable the children to change words and move them around before completing the final version.

Follow-up

After a brainstorming session, allow the children to write about a topic in the same way.

Books for all

Age range
Ten to eleven.

Group size
Four to six.

What you need
A word processor or a computer with a word-processing facility that produces a large infant-type print, scissors, drawing and colouring tools, adhesive, A4 sheets of paper.

Starting points
Ask the groups to investigate what young children read. They may need the cooperation of the teachers lower down the school. How many words are there on a page? Which words and pictures are frequently used? What are the stories about? Ask the children to do a simple survey on the most popular stories for five- and six-year-olds.

What to do
Have each group work as a team to create books for young children. They should draw the pictures and then produce the text on the word processor. Ask them to decide on the story and then, putting one or two lines to a page, print out and stick the story on to folded A4 sheets of paper, making an A5 booklet.

Follow-up
Let the children read the books to the younger children and collect comments on the story. Ask some of the younger children to read the books to check how easy they are to read.

Presentation

The possibilities for presenting children's work in a wide variety of interesting ways have grown rapidly with the development of Information Technology. Obviously, the more advanced your computer system and software package, the greater the possibilities for producing exciting presentations. However, whatever your computer system, there are always possibilities for improving the presentation of children's work.

You will need either a desk-top publishing (DTP) or a word-processing package which allows you to choose different print styles and sizes. A DTP package allows you to plan a page with various sections – one box or frame for the headline and others which allow graphics and text to be put on the page. Equally, a graphics package is very useful and there is a wide range of programs which allow you to experiment with text and pictures. You will obviously need a printer; a colour printer has many advantages but excellent results can be achieved with a humble, basic dot-matrix system.

If you use a word processor, print-outs may need to be cut and pasted in the traditional way on to a larger sheet of paper and possibly photocopied to achieve the final result. Desk-top publishing and more advanced packages allow you to cut and paste electronically on screen.

The possibilites provided by the computer for presenting children's work are important for a number of reasons. Firstly, because children have the chance to produce work to a high standard of presentation, you have the opportunity to raise their self-esteem. Work produced in a professional-looking format is often highly valued. Secondly, when children have to present work for an audience, you can encourage them to be constructively critical of their own work and that of others.

You can also encourage children to consider how best to approach a task; you can begin to move away from the situation where you provide the software to one where the child chooses the IT tool which he believes is best for the job.

Shaped writing

Age range
Eight to eleven.

Group size
Individuals or small groups.

What you need
A word processor or a computer with a word-processing facility.

Starting points
Shaped-writing activities give children the opportunity to think carefully about the choice of words and to be concise. Using a word processor for the initial drafting and the presentation enhances such work, making experimentation easier and producing visually accurate final results that all children can achieve.

Explain to the children that in shaped writing the words represent an object or concept, both in what they say and in how they appear. The writing can be prose or poetry. Show the children examples such as those below.

What to do
Encourage the children in their groups to brainstorm themes for writing. Almost any topic can be covered. It could be one that is currently being covered in class or one stimulated by outside interests and leisure activities. Ask the children to choose one theme and discuss ways of projecting it in shaped writing. With some thought

```
      A
     MER
    RYCHR
   ISTMAST
  OEVERYONE
 AMERRYCHRIS
TMASTOEVERYON
EANDAHAPPYNEWYE
      AR
      EV
      ER
      YO
      NE
```

```
      HAT
    HAT#HAT
      FA
  H   CE   H
DAARMBODYARMAD
 N   BODY   N
     BODY
     BODY
     BODY
     L  L
     #  #
     E  E
     #  #
  FOOTG GFOOT
```

```
          This
        is an oak
     tree. Many years
 ago they were grown in
huge forests so that there
  would be enough wood
    to build ships for
     the Royal Navy
           in
          the
          days
          when
         ships
          were
         built
          from
          wood
```

and ingenuity, most shapes are possible. The shape can even be filled in with extra characters such as # or $, as in the body example above.

A word processor that offers different sizes of type opens up even more possibilities. For instance, a piece of writing about the growth of a plant could be printed in gradually increasing letter sizes.

Follow-up
Shaped writing can make a very impressive wall display. Let the children mount their own display.

Hold the front page

Age range
Nine to eleven.

Group size
Two to six children.

What you need
A word processor or a computer with a word-processing facility or a desk-top publishing package. (Some programs give a ready-made layout of a front page but these are not essential to the activity), a printer, scissors, adhesive, paper.

Starting points
This activity can be treated as an exercise in itself and does not need to be part of a larger project. However, you could choose some themes from, say, a history project, and ask the children to write the front page

and the lead story of a momentous event, for example, NEW YORK TIMES, 'The *Titanic* Lost at Sea.' Alternatively, if you don't mind stretching credibility, ANCIENT BRITONS' GAZETTE, 'Romans Land In Force: Roman troops backed up by a squad of elephants today landed at . . .'

At this stage it is probably best to concentrate on one lead story for the front page. However, there is no reason why smaller articles could not be included as well.

What to do
Show the children a collection of front pages from a variety of newspapers, preferably published on the same day. Ask them to compare the papers. Do the tabloid press make one story dominate the whole page?

The larger newspapers have more space but does one story still dominate? How are photographs used to back up the lead story? Emphasise the fact that the front page is important because it helps people to decide which paper to buy.

Ask the children to choose a newspaper and analyse the contents of its front page. What does it consist of? Is the banner headline written to inform or grab the attention of the reader? How does the presentation grab your attention? Is the headline linked to a striking or startling photograph? Ask the children to consider if the layout and presentation of the page is as important as the contents.

Simulate a news office by giving the children information about a story. (This could be linked to project work.) You could simulate information coming through by teletext or fax to the newsroom by feeding groups of children information written on pieces of paper. Ask some children to be reporters who write the stories and ask others to concentrate on the layout and final appearance of the front page.

Using the word processor or DTP, ask the children to build up their front page from this information. If you have a DTP package, ask the children to enter the text either on the word processor and then load it into the DTP package or encourage them to type it straight into the DTP program. Let them edit work as new information arrives. With a word processor, encourage the children to edit the stories when they have been printed off and before they are cut and pasted on to a larger sheet.

Follow-up

- Allow the children to display their front pages. Discuss with them how the front pages compare.
- Use the following activities in this chapter to investigate other aspects of newspapers.

Feature writer

Age range

Nine to eleven.

Group size

Two to six children.

What you need

A word processor or a computer with a word-processing facilities or a DTP package, a printer, a collection of newspapers, magazines and brochures, adhesive, scissors, paper.

Starting points

Investigate a variety of magazines and newspapers with the children. Ask them to find the various features such as the fashion page, gardening page, motoring page and so on.

What to do

In groups, ask the children to choose a feature page which they would like to create. This could reflect the children's own interests but try not to end up with all the boys being motoring correspondents and the girls looking after the fashion page! Mixed groups may be a good idea. Let them investigate newspapers and magazines for examples of the styles of layouts for their particular feature. How much space does the feature cover? Do the correspondents always investigate new developments? Does the motoring page always have a new model of car on it? Does it cover features such as winter driving? Is there a place for small items of news? What part do photographs play in the layout?

Give the children sufficient information to help them compile their article, for example, car brochures, recipes and fashion pictures. Make sure they have plenty of visual material either in the form of photos, sketches or disk-based copies of computer graphics.

Using a word processor or DTP package, ask the children to compile their feature page, editing on screen, in the case of a DTP program, or using traditional cut-and-paste techniques with a word processor. Emphasise the importance of using pictures on the page and if you have a DTP package, help them to make the most of the computer graphics.

Follow-up

- Let the children combine their features into a wall display.
- Help the children to create specialist magazines and journals based on, for example, the motoring or fashion industries.

Sports page

Age range

Nine to eleven.

Group size

Two to six children.

What you need

A word processor or a computer with a word-processing facility or a DTP package, a printer, scissors, adhesive, paper.

Starting points

With the children, look at a variety of newspapers and see how much space they devote to sports. Which sports are given most coverage? Are there other forms of sports news other than match reports? Are minority sports covered? Is the coverage factually based or are some stories used to grab attention? Does the back page resemble the front page with a headline and a photograph dominating? Do photographs have a prominent place? Are there any in-depth interviews with sporting personalities?

What to do

With the help of the computer, ask each group to produce a whole page of sports news. The children could base their coverage on school and local sports. Be careful not to let the boys write only about football but let them give it a realistic amount of space. Ask the groups to write a report of at least two contrasting events and an in-depth article, possibly on the facilities offered at a local sports hall, the local swimming club, a junior football club and so on.

Encourage the children to draft and edit their reports and lead article and lay out their pages with headlines and pictures, if possible. Some children could write the reports while others could be responsible for the page layout. If you have a DTP package, invite the children to edit on screen. However, with a word processor let the children edit with the traditional cut-and-paste method.

Follow-up

- Invite the children to make a display of the finished pages.
- Encourage the children to create a sports magazine using the computer to compile the pages.

Television reviews

Age range

Nine to eleven.

Group size

Two to six children.

What you need

A word processor or a computer with a word-processing facility or a DTP package, a printer, a collection of newspapers and magazines, scissors, adhesive, paper.

Starting points

With the children, investigate the television pages in a variety of newspapers and magazines. Encourage them to look at the layout of the pages. Do they have a lead story? What is it based on? Are there interviews with leading celebrities? Are there reviews of new programmes? Are viewers' letters published?

What to do

In groups, ask the children to plan reviews of television programmes which are to be shown the following week. (It may be best to restrict them to children's television.) Make sure they do a thorough review; if it is a drama programme, ask them to comment on the acting and particular actors as well as the story-line. Suggest that they ask children from other classes to write short letters about programmes they like or dislike on television. Encourage the children to select which letters to publish and decide whether or not they need to be edited. Invite them to construct a lead article based on magazine interviews.

With the help of a computer, ask the children to draft, edit and construct a television review page. If you have a DTP package, encourage the children to edit on screen but, with a word processor, ask them to use traditional cut-and-paste techniques.

Follow-up

- Let the pupils arrange a display of their pages.
- Invite the children to create, with the help of a computer, specialist television, cinema or show business magazines.

Editorial comment

Age range

Nine to eleven.

Group size

Two to six children.

What you need

A word processor or a computer with a word-processing facility or a DTP package, a printer, a collection of newspapers and magazines, a collection of stories (made up by you or from magzines).

Starting points

With the children, look at the various editorials in newspapers. What do they set out to do? Do they report the news or comment on it? Why do newspapers need an editorial? Emphasise that in the editorial the editor usually seeks to influence the reader in one way or another.

What to do

Give the children a number of stories to read. Ask them to choose a story to comment on and write an editorial. Ask each group to draft, discuss, revise and print the editorials, with the help of a computer. Explain that each editorial should carry a leading headline which reflects the tone of the passage. Encourage the children to revise their editorial on screen.

Follow-up

- Let the children display their editorials.
- Ask other children in the class to write letters to the editor, criticising the editorial. Let the editor then gauge if she is keeping the readership happy and frame answers or future comment accordingly.

Advertisements

Age range

Nine to eleven.

Group size

Two to six children.

What you need

A word processor or a computer with a word-processing facility or a DTP package, a printer, a collection of newspapers and magazines.

Starting points

With the children, examine the various types of advertisements in newspapers and magazines. These will range from large display-style advertisements which fill whole pages to small classified advertisements. The large ones are often dominated by large graphics with a simple headline message. Most newspapers have

columns of classified advertisements. Local newspapers feature pages of job, for sale and house advertisements.

What to do

Give each group plenty of magazines and newspapers to refer to. Offer them a choice of products and ask them to design with the help of a computer an advertisement for one of them. Clearly define how much available space they have (a quarter page or the bottom half of the right column on a two-column page, for example). Suggest that they use graphics but leave the choice to them. They could be photographs or computer graphics from a DTP package. Ask them to draft out headings, catch-phrases and short pieces of information on to the computer. Let each group discuss and edit their advertisement on the computer before completing the final version.

Follow-up

Ask the children to produce advertising posters for the school tuck shop, mini-enterprises, local shops and so on. Give them a specification of a market or audience for the advertisements. By using the computer, the children can constantly and easily revise their work to suit the changing criteria for the advertisement. For instance, the prices at the tuck shop may change; if the advertisement has been saved on disk, it can be easily edited.

Simple newspapers

Age range

Nine to eleven.

Group size

Two to six children.

What you need

A word processor or a computer with a word-processing facility or a DTP package, a printer, a collection of newspapers and magazines, scissors, adhesive, paper.

Starting points

You could use this activity after having worked on some of the earlier activities on newspapers. Let the children study some real newspapers. Discuss with them the various parts of the newspaper and how certain people are responsible for producing different parts of the paper while others concentrate on putting the whole thing together. Suggest that they produce their own newspaper along the same lines, using a computer to help. Producing a first edition of a school magazine would be a useful vehicle for this activity.

If you have a full DTP package, the children can enter text either into a word processor and then load it into the DTP package or type it straight into the DTP program. (It is preferable to produce articles on separate word processors if possible.) The editing stage in this case can be done on screen using electronic forms of cut and paste. If you do not have a DTP package, let the children edit their articles using scissors and adhesive. The same concepts of page layout apply whichever method is used.

What to do

Ask each group to choose which one should be in charge of lead articles, editing, editorials, sports, features or advertising. Explain that each group will be responsible for planning, drafting, revising and producing finished 'copy' for the editorial team. Let the teams concerned discuss draft copies of articles and pages before passing them to the editorial team. Any changes can be made immediately on the computer. Once the copy has been written, ask the editorial team to begin to lay it out, make minor alterations or ask for major changes from the initiators, if required.

Follow-up

Invite the children to produce a half-termly magazine with an official deadline and publishing date.

Posters

Age range

Nine to eleven.

Group size

Small groups or pairs.

What you need

A word-processing package, a graphics package, a DTP package or specialist poster designing program, a variety of posters, paper, felt-tipped pens, glue, scissors.

Starting points

Show the children a variety of posters and discuss what the posters were designed for. How are the posters laid out? What do the posters consist of? How are words displayed? How are visual images used? Which are the most eye-catching posters?

What to do

Tell the children that they are to create a poster with the help of a computer. This could be a poster for an event, such as the school fête or a PTA coffee morning. Alternatively, it could advertise the school tuck shop or the lunch-time computer club. Let the children sketch out a few ideas on paper and then start designing the poster at the computer.

If you have a word processor it must be able to print out text in a variety of sizes and styles. Suggest that the children print out each style of text separately and then paste them together later. Graphics packages often handle text in a variety of interesting ways; the children may be able to 'fill' text with a variety of colours or

display text upside down or on its end. With a DTP package or specialist poster program, the children will be able to design the program on screen from scratch. Encourage them to create a large poster and assemble it from a collection of sequenced computer print-outs.

Follow-up

- Let the children display their posters around the school, if appropriate.
- Encourage other members of staff to commission posters from your children. Ask the children to design and draft out their proposals before going back to the teacher to have the work checked so that it meets his requirements.

Bordered writing

Age range
Six to eleven.

Group size
Small groups or individuals.

What you need
A writing package which allows you to use, make or select page borders – a variety of these programs are available, of different complexity and type. Some programs present you with a single screen, bordered with patterns or pictures. Others allow you to choose a surround from a variety of pre-prepared choices. Another type allows you to construct your own border from a variety of pictures and symbols; a printer.

Starting points
Discuss with the children the idea of writing a piece of poetry or prose and then decorating it with an attractive border. Ask them if they think this would enhance their

work. Ensure that you have some prepared borders or the resources to construct suitable borders to accompany children's poems or prose based on particular themes.

What to do

Introduce a theme for the children to base their writing on. Use the computer to show the children the range of borders available and how to display them on screen. Let the children consider the type of border they would choose for their writing. A colourful border would obviously not suit writing on a night-time theme.

Borders have several advantages for presenting work done by children who use words with difficulty. A few sentences surrounded by a border can look like a completed piece of work; the same few sentences on an empty sheet may well look a little less consequential.

Allow the children to compose their text away from the computer but with short pieces of writing, and especially short poems, it should be possible for them to work at the keyboard. Moving or replacing words is so much quicker on a computer. You may need to ensure that they save their work on disk and come back to it at a later date. If you have a colour printer this may take some time to print out; save the work and print it off at lunchtime or after school.

Follow-up

Bind the children's pieces of work together to produce a book of bordered pages.

Picture caption

Age range
Six to eleven.

Group size
Pairs or individuals.

What you need
A word processor or a computer with a word-processing facility or a DTP package, a printer.

Starting points
There are two types of program which allow you to approach this activity. One loads a prepared screen which has areas set aside for children to enter text; the other type allows you to enter text and then place pictures on to the writing screen.

The first type of program can prove very useful, for example, children can actually write about their day at the beach on to a picture of a beach. Some screens can be set up so that the text gradually fills the screen. For example, if the children write about a journey into space on a screen showing planets, the more they write, the more the planets are blacked out.

The second type of program allows children to mix pictures and text more freely. For young children, you can load a picture on to the screen and ask them to write something about it. A child could choose a picture of an animal and then write a sentence or two about it underneath. Alternatively, you could let the child enter some text and then select and arrange illustration(s) for her work.

What to do
Invite the children to create captions or short stories to accompany pictures on the computer screen. Use the computer to demonstrate how to load up prepared pages or to load pictures on to the screen (depending on which type of programme you have chosen). Allow the children to experiment freely, drafting and editing their text. If they make a real mess, they can always load up the screen and pictures again from disk. Teach the children how to save and load their work so that they do not need to finish it in one attempt. If you have a colour printer, leave the printing until after school or lunchtime.

Follow-up
Collect the children's work into a folder or bind it together to make a class book.

Letter-headed notepaper

Age range
Nine to eleven.

Group size
Pairs or small groups.

What you need
A DTP package or word-processing facility which includes a variety of fonts or type sizes, a selection of headed notepaper, a printer, paper, pencils.

Starting points
Show pupils the type of headed notepaper that companies and organisations use. Include the school's notepaper. Discuss why they use headed notepaper and what techniques are used to highlight the name, address, important personnel and so on. How are most letterheads composed?

What to do
Ask the pupils to compile rough drafts and ideas for headed notepaper for their class, school or an invented or historical organisation. Let them do this on paper away from the computer. At the computer, encourage them to create the first versions of letterheads and print them off. Ask the children to test out the letterheads on staff or other pupils and refine their ideas. Let them use the finished letterheads for correspondence in another project. Suggest that the class use their own letterhead for notes and general correspondence.

Follow-up
Ask other members of staff to commission headed notepaper from your class. Tell them to make alterations to the draft versions as it is a valuable part of the exercise for your children to edit the headings until they are exactly as required.

Folder front and dividers

Age range
Nine to eleven.

Group size
The whole class, individuals or groups.

What you need
A graphics package, a word-processing facility with a variety of type sizes and fonts or a DTP package, a printer, paper, scissors, adhesive.

Starting points

This activity is ideal if your class is engaged on a project and is producing either an individual or a class folder to present at the end of the project. Explain that the aim is to design and produce front covers and section dividers for project work.

What to do

Explain to the class that the front cover of the folder should reflect the project as a whole. After discussing with the children the nature and aims of the project, let them choose the print style and graphics to use. They could produce the graphics in traditional ways and use the computer to provide print-outs of headings which they could cut out and paste together. The cover need not have any graphics, or the children may decide to use a small logo; alternatively, a large piece of graphics may dominate the whole cover.

Suggest that section dividers may be more functional. The children may choose to design these using a large heading in a uniform print style, for instance. If the whole class is working on the design of the folder, split them up, with one group working on the front cover while pairs of children design a particular section divider.

Ensure that the children are actively engaged in discussions at every design stage. The beauty of using the computer is that changes are always possible at any stage in the process. For instance, if the title needs rewording, resizing or repositioning, the children can do this quite easily without having to start again from a new piece of paper.

Follow-up

Suggest that the children design project folder fronts and dividers for other classes in the school.

Invitations

Age range
Six to eleven.

Group size
Pairs or small groups.

What you need
A graphics package, a DTP package or a word-processing facility, a printer, a collection of invitations.

Starting points
Show the children a collection of printed invitations such as formal wedding invitations and birthday party invitations. Discuss with the children what sort of information an invitation contains.

What to do
Ask the children to design an invitation for a particular event, for example, an eight-year-old's birthday party which is to be held at a local community centre. Give them information such as the time, date and venue. Let the children choose how to arrange this information on the invitation. Suggest that they use a graphics or writing package, depending on what you have. Encourage them to draft, save, redraft and print off their ideas.

Return the invitations another day and tell the children that the venue and type of party has changed. It is now to be held at the local sports hall and will be a swimming party. Suggest that they could totally rewrite their invitation or issue a covering note outlining the changes.

Follow-up
Let the children consider the type of invitation required for more formal occasions, for example, inviting the Lord Mayor to their school's summer fair.

Tickets

Age range
Nine to eleven.

Group size
Pairs or small groups.

What you need
A DTP package, a graphics or word-processing package, a printer, a collection of tickets to a variety of events.

Starting points
Show the children tickets for a variety of events. Discuss with them the arrangements of graphics, logos and print styles.

What to do
Let the children choose an event to design tickets for. This could be the school play, an important sports fixture and so on. Let them decide roughly how big the tickets should be and how many would fit on to a page of A4 paper.

Using the computer, let the children design, save and print off a ticket. Discuss with them whether it is really suitable and whether it could be improved. After they have agreed on a finished product, let them investigate the possibility of copying the ticket several times on one page to produce a master page to photocopy.

Follow-up
Arrange for the children to design and produce the tickets for a forthcoming school event. Make sure the headteacher or organising teacher inspects draft ideas at various stages of development and that the finished product is as near as possible to what is required.

Making pictures

A computer can perform many different functions depending on the software that is used. In this chapter, the activities use graphics or drawing packages to help you introduce your children to computer art and design. The use of graphics packages supports the Communication Strand of Information Technology in the National Curriculum.

There are three basic types of graphics packages available.

- The first of these allow the child to build up a picture from pre-prepared resources. The screen has a background on which children can add smaller images, sometimes with the aid of a concept keyboard or a mouse. This type of package is very useful for early years pupils, those with special needs or children not confident enough to create a picture for themselves.
- The second type of package has pre-prepared shapes which children can manipulate on a blank screen. The shapes can be chosen, changed and arranged to produce a picture or design. This type of package is useful for children who are ready to produce their own design but not yet ready to tackle a blank screen.
- The third type of package allows complete freedom for drawing. The programs are very extensive and almost anything is possible. Depending on the package, the user is offered a selection of tools to create a design or picture. Most packages allow a mouse or tracker ball to be used to manipulate either straight or curved lines on the screen. Once the parts of the picture have been drawn, they can be coloured in with the available colour selection or new colours can be mixed. Some packages offer a selection of shapes that can be chosen, sized and placed on the screen as necessary.

When children have worked on a graphics package, let them print off a copy of their work. Most graphics

packages allow colour printing to a colour printer. Although it is not essential, a colour printer enhances work by giving a more realistic representation of the work. For certain colour printers, special ink cartridges are available which allow the print-out to be ironed on to fabric, thereby giving the work another purpose. It is also possible to print on to transfers which can decorate pottery.

The following activities are designed to help you use these different types of graphics packages depending on the age and ability of the children. Although ideas are given for each activity, the content of the graphics created can generally be changed to suit your topic.

As only pairs or small groups will be involved at the computer at any one time, you will need to occupy the other children. Some of the activities will require follow-up work away from the computer; other activities need to be planned before the computer is used.

Emphasise that the children should negotiate computer time with each other and realise that they all need the opportunity to try out and develop ideas. This is where the saving of work to disk is so important. Point out that they do not necessarily have to finish an activity in one session, but that the work can be spread over a period of time. With print-outs, the children can reflect at the end of each session how their work has progressed and where alterations or enhancements can be made during the next session.

A story scene

Age range
Five to seven.

Group size
Small groups.

What you need
A graphics package that provides a scene and the possibility of adding smaller pictures to it, a printer, a story that can be illustrated by the program you have chosen (this can be a published one or one that you have made up for the purpose).

Starting points
Tell the story to the children and then discuss it with them. Encourage them to talk about what images the story brought to mind.

What to do
Invite the children to illustrate the story on the computer using computer graphics. Load the computer program and put the background scene on to the screen. Show the children the smaller pictures that they can add to the background screen and demonstrate how to do it.

Let the children build up the picture which fits the story you have told. Invite them to tell the story as they do so. With the children's help, print out the completed scene.

Follow-up
- Let the children use a word processor to retell the story to put with their printed picture.
- Make a set of sequenced story cards and let the children build a picture on the computer, either by reading the cards themselves or by having someone read the cards to them.
- Make a set of counting cards asking the child to put the correct number of objects on to the screen.
- Let the children write a story and illustrate it on the computer.
- Create a picture on the screen and ask the children to tell the story of the picture while you write it down.

A shape person

Age range
Five to seven.

Group size
Pairs.

What you need
A graphics program that allows the children to alter shapes on a blank screen to create a picture or design, a printer.

Starting points
Discuss with the children the names of the shapes that are available in the program. Talk about the shapes and their properties, for example, the number of sides, number of corners and the number of angles.

What to do
Show the children how to use the program, how to manipulate the shapes on the screen and how to change the regular shapes of square, circle, hexagon, triangle and the length of the line by making them bigger or smaller, turning them, squashing and stretching them and colouring them in. Let the children make a person from the given shapes, save it to disk and print it out.

Follow-up
- Let the children use a word processor to write a story about their shape person.
- Invite the children to make a vehicle from shapes, for example, a bus, a lorry or a yacht.
- Ask the children to use the program to create a new vehicle.
- Talk with the children about the class topic and let them create a picture associated with it.
- Show the children how to edit a picture by covering the incorrect shape with the same shape and then colouring it in with the background colour. This, in effect, erases the shape.

Designer planet

Age range

Five to nine.

Group size

Pairs or small groups.

What you need

A graphics program that allows the children to alter shapes or a free-drawing package, a screen with a large empty circle on it, a printer, pictures of the planets.

Starting points

Talk with the children about the planets in our solar system and show them pictures of them. Discuss with them the ideas of a new planet and what they think it would look like.

What to do

Invite the children to design a planet on the computer. Load the computer program and the screen with a large empty circle. Ask the children to colour in the planet. Let them put different shapes on to the planet and colour them in. Alternatively, ask them to draw areas on the planet and colour these in.

Follow-up

- Ask the children to explain what the different shapes and coloured areas on the planet represent.
- Let the children imagine they are actually on the planet and ask them to tell the rest of the class about life there. Ask them to draw pictures of what they can see on the planet, including any inhabitants.

Shadows

Age range
Six to nine.

Group size
Pairs or small groups.

What you need
A graphics package that allows the children to alter shapes or a free-drawing package, a printer.

Starting points
Talk to the children about shadows. Go out into the playground on a sunny day to let them see their shadows.

What to do
Using the computer, let the children draw a picture of themselves in colour. Now ask them to use the program to draw a shadow of themselves on the same screen. Ask them to colour the shadow in black or another dark colour.

The graphics package will determine how the children create the shadow. With a simple package, they may have to completely redraw the figure on a new area of the screen. With a more sophisticated package, they will be able to copy the original figure, rotate it and reposition it on the screen. Ask the children to save the picture to disk and print it out.

Follow-up
- Let the children draw the figure again and put the shadow in a different place.
- Ask them to draw other objects together with their shadows.
- Encourage the children to create a silhouette of the object drawn on the screen.
- Let the children draw other objects and their silhouettes.

Designer jumpers

Age range
Six to nine.

Group size
Pairs or small groups.

What you need
A free-drawing package that allows colours to be mixed, a screen with an outline of a jumper, a printer, a selection of patterned jumpers.

Starting points
Show the children a selection of patterned jumpers and talk about how the effects have been achieved. Discuss with them the idea of designing a jumper which would show that the wearer belongs to the school choir, chess club or recorder group.

What to do
Load the computer program and draw an outline of a jumper on the screen. Show the children how to use the program to mix their own colours. Let the children fill the

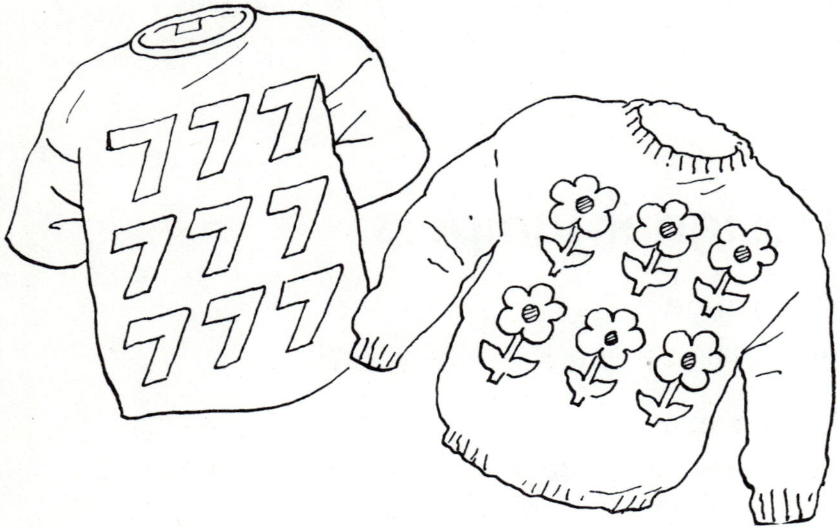

jumper with their own created colour pattern. Help the children to save the jumper design to disk and print it out.

Follow-up

- Suggest to the children that they pretend to be fashion designers, using computer technology to create their designs. Ask them to create designs for trousers, dresses, coats, skirts and so on. Initially, you may have to draw the outlines of the clothes but, with practice, the children may be able to draw their own outlines.
- Ask the children to design a new school uniform, using the computer. Let them print off the designs, display them where all the school can see them and ask the rest of the school for their comments.

The other half

Age range
Seven to nine.

Group size
Pairs.

What you need
A graphics package that allows the children to alter shapes or a free-drawing package, a screen with the left half of a symmetrical house, a printer.

Starting points
Discuss symmetry with the children. Ask them to find objects around the classroom which are symmetrical.

What to do
Tell the children that they are to do some work with symmetry on the computer. Load the picture of the half-completed symmetrical house on to the computer screen. Discuss with the children the properties of the picture. Ask them to remember what you have said

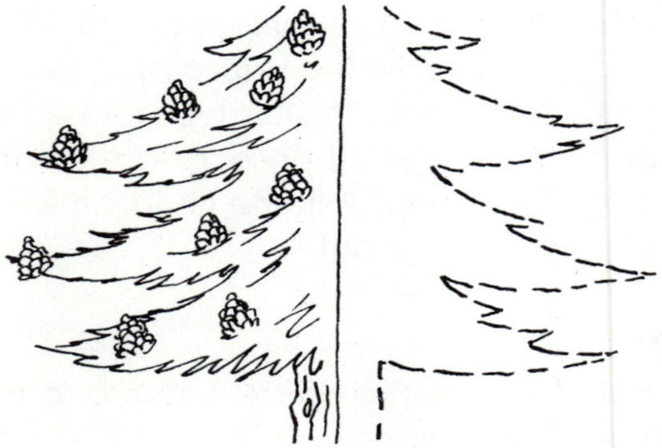

about symmetry and show them how to complete the house. Erase your work and ask the children to draw the other half of the house. Let the children save the picture to disk and print it out.

Draw one half of other symmetrical items such as a table, a flower or a clown's face and ask the children to complete the picture.

Follow-up

With the children's help, create a picture which has top-to-bottom symmetry and discuss with them the idea of reflection. If you have a free-drawing package, you may be able to show the children how to copy the original half of the picture, flip it and position it to complete the picture without actually drawing it.

3-D effects

Age range

Nine to eleven.

Group size

Pairs or small groups.

What you need

A selection of two-dimensional shapes and their 3-D equivalents, a free-drawing computer package, a printer.

Starting points

Talk with the children about two-dimensional shapes, in particular a square, and discuss their properties, such as

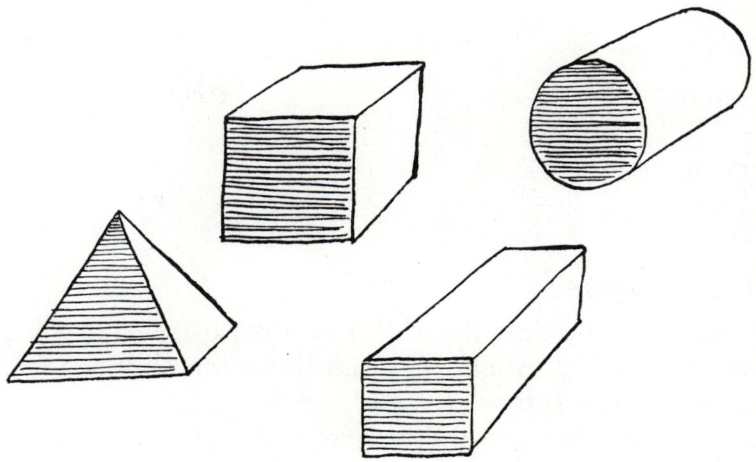

the number of sides, edges, angles and so on.

Introduce the three-dimensional shapes and talk about their properties. Include a cube among them.

What to do

Explain to the children that the computer can help them to understand three-dimensional shapes. Load the drawing package into the computer and allow the children to draw a square on the screen. Ask them to add lines to the square to make it appear on the screen like a three-dimensional box. Let the children save the picture and print it out.

Follow-up

- Ask the children to draw a three-dimensional house on the screen, using squares and a triangle for the roof.
- Invite the children to make a circle into a cylinder on the screen. Encourage them to turn this into a tunnel.

You've been framed

Age range

Seven to eleven.

Group size

Pairs or small groups.

What you need

Examples of borders the children have used to display work, a graphics package that allows the children to alter shapes or a free-drawing package, a printer, a piece of work for display, scissors, adhesive.

Starting points

Discuss with the children how they have previously created frames to surround work displayed on the walls. Introduce the idea of creating a frame or border on the computer.

What to do

Load your computer program and show the children the limits of the screen. Explain to them how the program works and ask them to create a border around the four edges of the computer screen. Ask them to save the border to disk so it can be used again in the future. Let them print out the border and use it to display on the wall or in a folder a piece of written or word-processed work which they have cut to size.

Follow-up

- Ask the children to create a border made up from shapes, letters or numbers.
- If your program allows it, let the children create a border from their own design, which they have created as a large design, by making it smaller and replicating it all around the border area.

Wallpaper and curtain design

Age range

Eight to eleven.

Group size

Pairs or small groups.

What you need

A free-drawing graphics package which allows you to resize and replicate a design on the screen, a printer, examples of co-ordinating wallpaper and curtain fabrics, pencils, crayons and drawing paper, pieces of card, scissors, a ruler, adhesive.

Starting points

Discuss with the children what patterns for wallpaper and curtains they would like to have in their bedrooms if they could create their own.

What to do

Explain to the children how the graphics package works and ask them to design a print for their wallpaper and curtains. Once this is done, show them how to use the graphics package to make the original design smaller. Show them how to repeat the smaller version on the screen. Allow the children to print out two copies of their design.

Ask them to stick the print-out of the smaller design on to the same-sized piece of card. Explain that this will represent the wallpaper on one wall of their room. On a small piece of paper (for example, 5cm by 5cm), let them draw an outdoor scene. Ask them to stick this in the middle of the wall for the window.

Invite the children to make the pelmet and curtains from the print-out of the larger design. Let them cut a narrow strip from the print-out and stick it to a piece of card cut to the same size to make the curtain pelmet. Let them cut the rest of the print-out vertically into two and fold each one to look like undrawn pleated curtains. Ask them to stick one at each end of the pelmet and then stick the pelmet above the windows.

Follow-up

- It is possible to buy special ink cartridges for some colour printers that allow the pattern to be ironed on to fabric. If you have this facility, ask the children to make designs for fabric which they can use to decorate models or to make clothes for toys.
- Ask the children to make a motif for the wallpaper and curtains, such as a shape, a favourite character, a flower or a child's name. The design for the curtains could differ slightly from that for the wallpaper.
- Encourage the children to design and make a roller blind instead of curtains for the window.

Identikit pictures

Age range

Eight to eleven.

Group size

Individuals.

What you need

A free-drawing package that will allow the use of a digitizer; a digitizer (a digitizer is an interface which is either a separate piece of hardware attached to the computer by a lead or an integral part of the computer. It allows a video camera to be attached to the computer so that images captured by the camera can be displayed on the computer screen. This allows images to be saved on to a computer disk for re-use.); a video camera, a printer, scissors.

Starting points

Discuss with the children how photofit pictures are made up to help catch criminals. Explain that the photofit is made up in sections, such as the hair, eyes, nose, lips, chin and so on.

What to do

Tell the children that they are going to make photofit pictures with the help of the computer. Set up the computer with the graphics package, video camera and digitizer.

Using the video camera, take pictures of all the children's faces and save them on a disk. With the children's help, print out the children's digitized face pictures. Ask the children to cut their pictures into sections like a photofit picture.

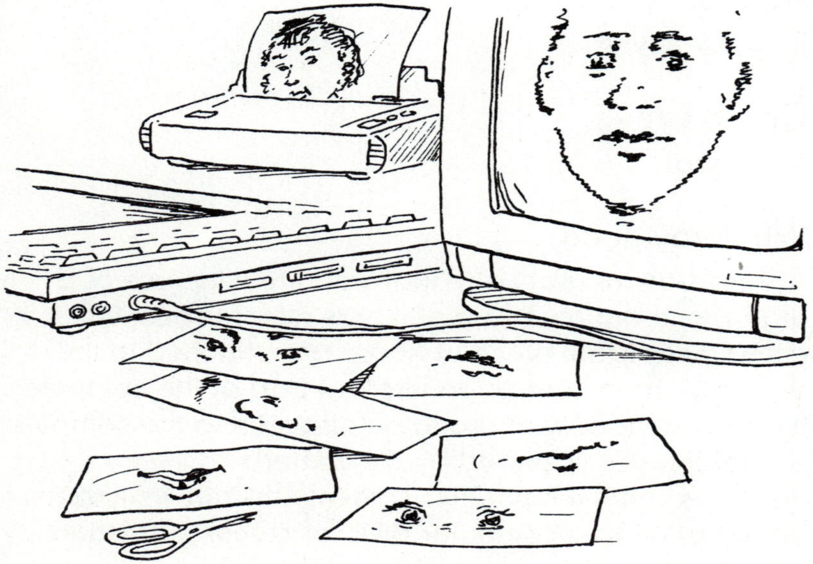

Follow-up

- Mix up the sections of the faces and ask the children to reassemble each other's pictures.
- Invite the children to make funny faces by deliberately putting wrong sections together.
- Ask the children to print out their digitized face pictures again and let them stick them on to large pieces of paper to make 'Wanted' posters by adding suitable text to the poster. Encourage the children to use the word processor or to create the text and then cut and paste it on to the poster.
- Let the children reload their digitized face picture on to the computer screen and use the graphics program to add features to it, such as a red nose, glasses, a beard and even a small body. Ask them save this version of their face to disk and print it out.

Logos galore

Age range

Seven to eleven.

Group size

Pairs or small groups.

What you need

A free-drawing graphics package, special colour inks (not essential), a printer.

Starting points

Ask the children to collect items that have logos. Discuss with the children what logos mean to them. Logos can

influence what we buy, particularly on sportswear and clothes. Ask the children what sort of logo they would like to attach to something important to them.

What to do

Allow the children to design their own logo using the graphics package at the computer. Explain that it could be a word or words or it could be a small motif or a combination of both. Remind them that the shape of the logo and the colours used are as important as the motif or words.

Let the children print out the logo as many times as necessary. If you have special inks in your printer which allow the design to be transferred on to fabric, let the children experiment with pieces of fabric or even old T-shirts.

Follow-up

- Let the children make a canvas bag and then apply or sew on their logo.
- Ask the children to make a logo for a club that they belong to, either in school or out of school.
- Hire a badge-making kit and let the children use their logos, printed out to the correct size, to make badges.

Stencil making

Age range

Nine to eleven.

Group size

Pairs.

What you need

A graphics package that allows children to alter shapes or a free-drawing package, a printer, sheets of card, paints, adhesive, scissors, fabric.

Starting points

Discuss with the children the idea of printing on to fabric using a stencil.

What to do

Allow the children to create a picture or design on the computer screen using the graphics package. Suggest that they limit the number of colours they can use, only three or four to begin with. Once the design is complete, ask them to print it out as many times as the different colours they have used. Let them stick the print-outs on to separate pieces of card. Ask them to cut out the same colours from each of the print-outs, for example, all the red colours from the first and all the green colours from the second and so on until they have a complete set of stencils. If the print-outs are black and white, ask them to cut the varying shades of grey from each one.

Let the children use the stencils on fabric, placing each stencil in the same place on the fabric but using a different colour each time for each stencil.

Follow-up

- As the children become more used to the technique, ask them to create more complex pictures using many colours but remind them that it must be possible to cut out the colours.
- Encourage the children to use the cut-out parts of the stencil placed on fabric or paper and paint over them to create the negative view of the design.
- Invite the children to use a large piece of fabric to create a backdrop or quilt. Suggest that they use the stencils alternately the right way up and upside down to create different effects.

Design planning

Age range
Eight to eleven.

Group size
Pairs.

What you need
A free-drawing graphics package, a printer, examples of design plans.

Starting points
Discuss with the children how architects always create a flat design on paper before actually constructing anything. Show them examples of design plans. Talk with the children about scale and the need to scale carefully a design plan so that on actual construction everything fits into its correct place. Ask them to suggest

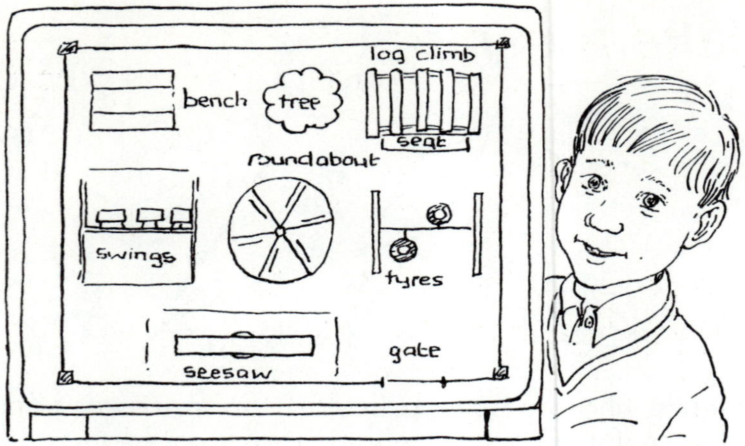

amenities they would like to see in a children's park if they could design one.

What to do
Using the computer, ask the children to design a park with all its amenities and to print it out. Remind them to bear in mind scale as they design their park.

Follow-up

- Ask the children to build their park from junk materials.
- Suggest that the children design the plans for a luxury home, taking into account all the storeys of the house.
- Let the children draw the plans on the computer for the school buildings.
- Ask the children to draw the plans for something associated with the current class topic.
- If your computer program allows objects on the screen to be moved, suggest that the children draw a plan of the classroom and its contents and then move the furniture to different parts of the room. Can they use the classroom floor space more efficiently?

Make a game

Age range
Nine to eleven.

Group size
Pairs or small groups.

What you need
Examples of board games, a free-drawing computer package, a printer, card, adhesive, scissors.

Starting points
Show the children the board games and talk with them about them. Are all the squares on the board different or are some the same? Create a new board game with the children, taking care how the squares on the board will look.

What to do
Load the computer program and allow the children to create the squares for the board game. The computer program should allow them to create squares larger than the final ones will be. These can then be sized down so that each of the final squares is the same size. This will make construction of the final board game easier. Let the children save each square of the board game to disk so that the repeated squares can be printed out later, without having to redraw them.

Ask the children to print out the board game squares as they are completed. Invite them to cut them out and glue them on to a piece of card large enough to take all the squares. Let the children try out their game on their friends.

Follow-up
Encourage the children to make a board game with different-shaped playing areas such as circles, hexagons or octagons.

Databases

The information-handling strand of Information Technology (IT) in the National Curriculum states that children should collect information and store it on a database. They should be able to retrieve it, add to it, make corrections and then use the database to provide information and test hypotheses. However, before you start to use a database, it is important to know what a basic package should offer and why information handling is an important part of the IT Attainment Target.

There are different types of database but the one referred to in this chapter is the relational database which is based on the card index system, where a card becomes a record on the database and the headings on the card are called fields.

Databases, like most other packages, come in all forms and because of memory problems on many computers, facilities provided in one package are not necessarily present in another. However, a database must include the following main facilities:

- an easy method of setting it up;
- an easy method of entering the data and changing it, if necessary;
- the facility to save, reload, add data and edit data easily;
- the facility to sort information into alphabetical or numerical order quickly;
- the facility to search the database for specific records and then to keep these records in a subset in order to add to or narrow down the search;
- facilities to produce graphs of information obtained in a search;
- the facility to print the results of a sort or search and any graphs produced.

Although most databases will provide these facilities, many have limitations that can be very restricting, for

instance, limitations on the number of fields or records that can be held. It is important, therefore, to seek advice from people who use databases before buying one. The question of why we use a database can be answered by the fact that it can quickly sort items into order and produce graphs. But it has far more uses than these in the classroom. It can demonstrate in a practical way how larger databases are used in real-life situations. For example, there is seemingly little point in using a class database to search for the children who have blonde hair when all you have to do is look; but because the police can find in much the same way the owner of a set of fingerprints or a car registration number from a huge database, the children are learning how a database works.

In reality, most of the important work takes place away from the computer. What information should be collected? What do we want to know? A project on dinosaurs may throw up the question, 'Were the biggest dinosaurs meat- or plant-eaters and did they live on land or in water?' The ensuing collection of information would involve research and note-taking. With older children, gathering information on, for example, clothing materials, could be collected by interview, questionnaire or observation following an appraisal of the different methods.

As you enter information into the database, you must always be mindful of what the database is to do. Colour is an example of this. If you have a database of cars in which there is a field for colour, you may wish to determine the most popular colour. The best way to do this would be to look at a graphic representation of the colours. However, as a computer will only recognise words that are the same to put in a bar chart, it could not cope with the manufacturers' versions of colours. For example, the colour blue could be quartz blue, azure or moon with one company and balliol, wedgewood, aqua, tasman, matisse, bicayne or atlantic with another. To produce a sensible graph, these would have to be categorised as just blue or perhaps light and dark blue.

Searching for errors is a skill in itself. How do you find a spelling error in a database? Questioning the database may show the error but will it be recognised? It is therefore important to try to make sure that information is correct before it goes into the database. This can be done initially by children comparing their information with that of others and having a checker standing by the computer as they enter it. Children will learn the logic of an 'and' or an 'or' search as a result of careful problem-setting. These two major types of searches are best illustrated by a simple example. If you search a database about people for all those who have blonde hair <u>and</u> blue eyes you actually narrow the search to find only those people who have both attributes. If you search for the people who have blonde hair <u>or</u> blue eyes you widen the search to include people who have either attribute.

Careful questioning and discussion of graphical representations will enable children to acquire the ability to interpret graphs.

Birthdays

Age range
Six to seven.

Group size
The whole class or small groups with supervision.

What you need
A computer system, a simple graph-producing package or a database that can produce graphs, a large sheet of paper, squares of sticky paper in 12 different colours.

Starting points
There are literally hundreds of contexts for graphic display of information but it is best to start with something that is always of interest to all the children, for example, birthdays. Ask the children if they know which month they were born in. As each one answers, (and some may need your help), give them a square of coloured sticky paper with their name written on it. (Each month should have a different colour, if possible). When all the children have one, put a large sheet of paper listing the months in order on the wall. Make comparisons by questioning the children. 'Who has a red square?' 'How many children have their birthday in March?' Invite the children to stick their square on the sheet to produce a bar chart. When this is complete, carry out further language work such as bigger, biggest, more and most, and so on.

What to do
Introduce the computer to the children and taking the information from the chart on the wall, help the children

to enter into the graph package the months of the year followed by the number of children who have birthdays in that month. Show the children how quickly a bar chart can be produced. You may also be able to introduce the pie chart. Using the computer graph, ask the children questions such as when there are likely to be the most birthday parties. Pin up a printed copy of the chart next to the wall chart and ask the children whether or not they look the same.

Follow-up
With the children, collect and examine information regularly on a wide variety of topics. Ask the children to look at each other's eyes and produce a graph of eye colours. Other ideas are hair colours and favourite items such as food, zoo animals, pets and colours.

Exciting Victorian times?

Age range
Seven to eleven.

Group size
The whole class working in pairs.

What you need
A computer system, a database, access to a library or a large number of reference books.

Starting points
Begin this work during a study of the Victorians. Once the topic is well established, the children will begin to realise that there were many exciting developments during this period. However, to show their chronology in relation to other factors and events, suggest that they construct a database of each year of Queen Victoria's reign.

What to do

Let them give each record a year as its first field, for example, 1876. They can then choose the other fields from, for example, inventions, literature, discoveries, events, prime ministers, royal family, laws and world events. Alternatively, suggest that they build the databases on famous people who lived in Victorian times. The fields could be chosen from first name, surname, title, occupation, why they were famous, date or year of birth, date or year of death and age.

A database on the Victorian era can provide the answers to many questions. For example, ask the children to find out how many prime ministers there were during Victoria's reign. Who was prime minister for the longest period? A bar chart should give the answers to both these questions. Alternatively, if the children input information on famous people ask them to see if they can find another person who lived throughout Victoria's reign. In this case, they would have to search for those who were born before she became queen and outlived her.

Follow-up

Invite the children to produce a database covering the last 60 years, asking the question, 'Has it been as memorable as Victoria's reign?'

Traffic census

Age range

Eight to eleven.

Group size

Small groups.

What you need

A computer system, a graph-producing package, a road where children can observe traffic from a safe place, pencils, paper.

Starting points

If your school is close to a road, ask the children if they think the road is busy. What do we mean by busy? Can they guess how many cars travel along the road in an hour or a day?

What to do

If it is safe to do so, allow the children to watch the traffic on the road and write down how many different vehicles pass by in 15 minutes. Give the groups different times to collect their data so that a comparison can be made. Let each child be responsible for a different type of vehicle. (Discuss these before starting the activity to differentiate between a van, a lorry and an articulated

lorry.) Ask one child to be in charge of 'odd' vehicles, such as fire engines or tractors.

After the observation period, let the children count the number of vehicles and enter the totals into a graph-drawing package. Ask them which sort of vehicle uses the road most and least and whether any types of vehicles were not seen at all.

Follow-up

- Let older children collect another set of data, as well as a number count of vehicles. Give the child collecting the number of cars a list of colours and ask her to put a mark by the appropriate colour as each one passes. Also, ask the child counting the lorries or articulated lorries to count the wheels, and/or select from a set of possible loads, for example, food, furniture, building materials or machine parts.
- Encourage the children to build a database on cars. Ask them to carry out a survey of the cars belonging to families of children in school. Suggest that they ask questions to find out more about the colour, age, engine size and petrol type of cars in the area.

Land use in the High Street

Age range
Nine to eleven.

Group size
Pairs or small groups.

What you need
A computer system, a database, pencils, paper.

Starting points
Any topic which introduces local amenities or shops could lead to the question of what is in the High Street. This could be the main street in a town, a shopping complex or several streets within a small town, depending on the age of the children.

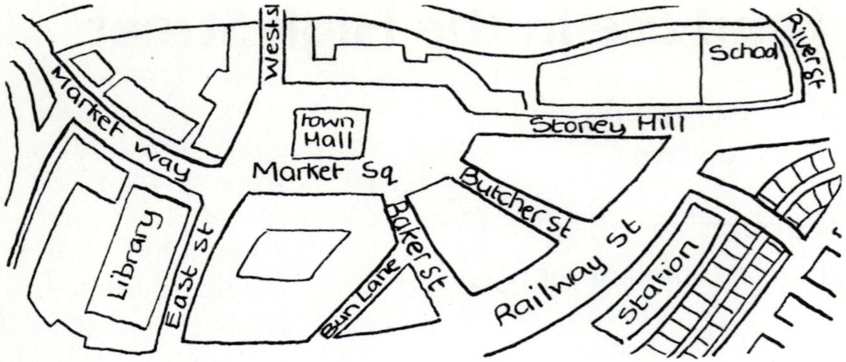

What to do

Discuss with the children the different types of building they might see in a high street and how they might be used. For example, a building that was originally a house may now be used as offices or as a flat with a small shop on the ground level. Take the children along the street to collect information on the buildings and to map the premises against what is on the other side of the road. Ask them to note the width of the building by simple pacing or by using a trundle wheel.

Ask the children to enter the data into a database, using fields such as road number, type (house, office, shop), use (building society, shoe shop), size and number of floors.

Follow-up

Let the children draw maps of the street and discuss with them what is missing. This could lead to them devising a local development plan. Where should a new building go and why? Which building must change to cater for it? Let the children consult local history documents to compare the present street with how it was some years ago. Which changes make it better and which ones make it worse?

The new community centre

Age range

Ten to eleven.

Group size

Pairs or small groups.

What you need

A computer system, a database, pencils, paper.

Starting points

Ask the children what they like to do in their spare time. Ask them to devise different headings to put them under. For instance, they could have outdoor sports, indoor sports, hobbies, clubs, entertainment, games and educational activities.

What to do

Tell the children to imagine that the council has decided to open a new community centre and is trying to find out what activities it should provide. Ask the children to plan a questionnaire that will give people the opportunity to request a range of different types of activities, not just sports. When the children have completed their questionnaires, ask them to decide on a final version which should combine the best ideas.

Invite each child to complete a questionnaire. Let them enter the information into the database. The fields on the database should be headings such as those suggested in the starting points. When the database is complete, ask the children to use the data to decide what the community centre should provide.

Follow-up

Invite the children to try the same questionnaire on adults and compare their findings. This should provoke a lot of discussion concerning provision for different ages, taking into consideration activities that may already be provided and how cost should be taken into account.

The weather

Age range

Eight to eleven.

Group size

Pairs or small groups.

What you need

A computer system, a database, equipment for measuring weather conditions.

Starting points

Question the children about the weather. Introduce the concept of measuring aspects of the weather. Ask questions such as, was it hot or cold yesterday? How cold? Was it colder than the day before? Which was the coldest day this week/month? How much rain fell? If it rains heavily for a few minutes, is it wetter than if it rains lightly all day? These questions could lead to a discussion about clouds and wind. Discuss the way the children would measure aspects of the weather and what equipment they would use.

What to do

With the children's help, set up equipment to measure weather conditions over a period of a month. Let them take maximum and minimum temperature readings for the school day. They should also measure rainfall. Where conditions cannot be measured, ask them to make a subjective textual entry, for example, the type of cloud cover. Ask them to update the database each day using fields such as rainfall, wind direction, sunshine hours and temperature highs and lows. If your database allows it, ask the children to compare average temperature or rainfall with records obtained from other sources.

Follow-up

Invite the children to collect further information for other months. If the database is powerful enough to hold a large number of records, let the children continue the topic for a year. There may be problems with collecting the information during holidays but this could be overcome with a little help from colleagues or parents.

The library

Age range
Ten to eleven.

Group size
Pairs and small groups.

What you need
A computer system, a database powerful enough to hold a large number of records.

Starting points
Ask the children what they know about libraries. Do they know how the books are ordered on the shelves? How can they find out if the library has a particular book which may not be on the shelf? Try to visit a library with the children to help them to understand the system. Identify the problem of trying to find a book by its name when the author is not known. Explain how a database might help and suggest that the children computerise their class library.

What to do
Ask the children to look at a book and write down information that they think would be useful in a database. This is usually found on the first two or three pages. Talk with the children about this and explain, where necessary, why the information is there and ask the children how useful it would be in their database.

Ask them to set up a database using field names chosen from the title, author, publisher, date of publication, date of last reprint, Dewey classification or ISBN number. This could be extended further by having

a field which describes whether the book is fiction, non-fiction or reference. They may also consider fields for date of purchase, type of cover (hard or paper), who takes out the book and the date taken. If a field is added for topics, ask the children to update the database when they find a book useful for the work they do. To begin with, let the children take turns in their groups to enter a number of books. Let them update the information on a rotation basis or when a child decides he can contribute to the record.

Many types of searches can be made on this type of database. A topic on Australia could involve a search such as 'title field contains Atlas OR topic field contains Australia'. This is a fairly easy 'or' search. A sort on the date of publication field could show which books may need to be replaced.

Follow-up
Ask the children to extend the database to the school library or even all the books in the school. If they do this, remind them to add a field to show where the book is normally found.

Ourselves

Age range
Eight to eleven.

Group size
Pairs or small groups.

What you need
A computer system, a database, equipment for measuring the children such as a scales, tape measure and a height measure.

Starting points
During a topic about ourselves or growth, ask the children to suggest ways in which they are different from each other. Ask them to write down as many as they can. Use their suggestions as a basis for the database.

What to do
With the children's help, design a data collection sheet based on the children's ideas about ourselves. They can be purely numerical, based on height and so on, or contain fields for eye and hair colour. Ask the children to include a field for age if they want to put themselves in age order. This will depend on the database but even with the most limited type, it is possible to enter a class of similarly aged children by entering a number based on the month, starting with September, or the month of birth of the oldest child.

Using the measuring equipment, ask the children to measure each other. Offer them a selection of measurements to take such as height, weight, foot size, head size, hand-span, arm-span (like a bird's wingspan) and waist. Let them use these measurements as the field names. If you include fields for vertical jump and horizontal jump, discuss with them how to establish fair testing. The best way of testing vertical jump is to ask a child to reach as high as possible to touch a wall which has measurements marked on it and then to ask her to jump to see how much higher she can reach. A horizontal jump is measured by how far a child can jump from a standing start with both feet together.

When the children have finished measuring, ask them to put the measurements into the database. Spotting mistakes is usually fairly easy in this type of database as a wrong entry usually stands out in a graph.

Many searches can be made but if the database can produce averages, ask the children to find those of shorter-than-average height who can jump higher than the class average and so on.

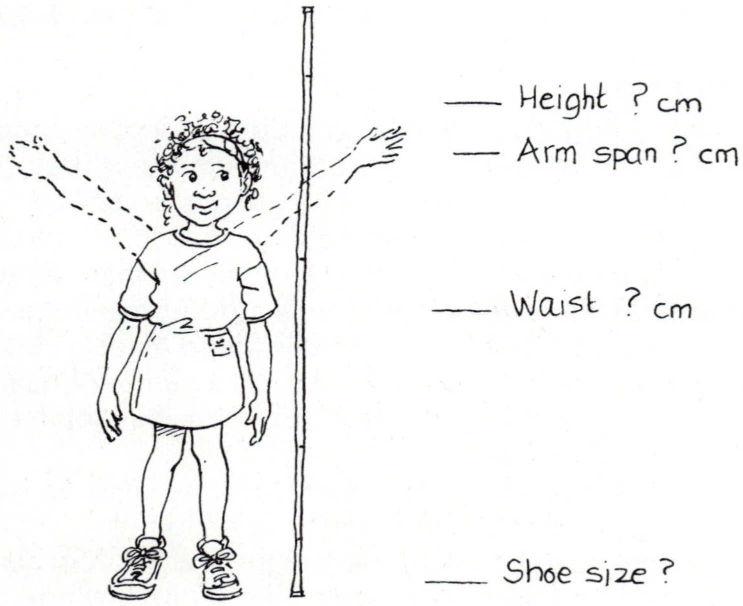

Follow-up

With older and more able children, it is possible to test hypotheses. Suggest that they investigate ideas such as the tallest children can jump the highest, the heaviest children are born in the summer and the highest jumpers can also jump the farthest.

Tudors and Stuarts

Age range

Eight to eleven.

Group size

Pairs or small groups.

What you need

A computer system, a database, reference books, a blackboard, chalk.

Starting points

Children involved in a topic on the Tudors and Stuarts soon realise that they have to deal with a number of kings and queens. Remembering who reigned when and matching events to the different reigns is always quite difficult. To help them, let them put the information into a database.

Begin by asking the children questions about the monarchs and the events that took place during their reign. When they find events difficult to remember, suggest that they produce a database containing this information, perhaps for others to use in the future.

What to do

Ask the children to suggest details which they might need to know about a monarch and write these on a board. Let the children produce a data collection sheet for keeping the information. Keep the number of fields fairly small so that the children, in their groups, can produce a sheet for each of the kings and queens. Suggest that the main fields are name, family, year of birth, year of accession, year of death, manner of death and main event during their reign.

Depending on the children's ability, the main events could be given more fields and categorised into areas such as military, exploration, world and so on. Older children will enjoy the challenge of finding these for themselves. Ensure that each group enters part of the data.

With the completion of the database, questions such as who reigned the longest and which family has the most kings and queens can be easily answered. Ask the children to carry out a more difficult 'and' search by looking at the monarch who reigned the longest and was a Stuart. Explain that the use of 'not' in the question can be shown if they ask which monarch did not die of old age.

Follow-up

- Ask the children to use the information gathered to produce a time-line. Hang up a string at child height across the classroom and ask the children to peg cards with the monarchs' name on them at appropriate points along the string. They can then peg other cards in place.
- Use the time-line as a quiz where you give the children a card and they have to peg it in the correct place.

Spreadsheets

A spreadsheet is an electronic version of the type of paper sheet which is still sometimes used to record financial accounts. It consists of a number of cells which are arranged in a grid of rows or columns. A number, word or formula can be entered into any of the cells. For example, a class may construct a spreadsheet to keep track of the stock in the school tuckshop:

	A	B	C	D
1	Item	Number	Cost	Total
2	Crisps	3	200	600
3	YoYos	3	150	450
4	Cola	4	220	880
5	Chews	3	145	435
6				2365

In the above spreadsheet the prices have been entered in pence and the number of stock is in boxes or cases. The cells of a spreadsheet are identified by a grid reference. In this example, the cost of each case of crisps is held in cell C2 while the total value of stock is held in cell D6. Not all the items listed in a spreadsheet are numbers; many words or labels are also included. Formulas consist of calculations, for example, in the above example, cell D2 holds the product of multiplying the contents of cell B2 by the contents of cell C2. Cell D6 holds the result of a formula to find the sum of the column of cells D2 to D5.

However, a spreadsheet is more than a clever calculator. If the price of a case of cola went up, the spreadsheet would recalculate all the other calculations dependent on it as soon as the new price is entered.

This type of software offers plenty of scope for children to model the way companies arrange their accounts. It also provides an ideal opportunity for you to set up problem-solving exercises within your classroom. The activities in this chapter, as well as working well on their own, will provide you with further ideas of using spreadsheets with children.

Water use

Age range

Eleven and over.

Group size

Small groups.

What you need

A computer system, a simple spreadsheet, pencils, paper, water, a one-litre measuring jug, a cassette recorder.

Starting points

Explain to the children that a spreadsheet is a manipulative tool and not just a database. Point out that its power lies in the speed of recalculation when some part of it is altered. Outline how a spreadsheet is particularly useful when calculating the variation of a consumable resource, such as water, and that it could be used to model other similar problems.

What to do

Ask the children to write down how water is used in their homes. When they have a list, ask them to order the uses from the greatest to the least. Discuss their findings with the children and let them compare their ideas of how many litres we use for various activities with the more realistic amounts. It is a good idea to have a one-litre container available for measuring amounts of water.

Set up the spreadsheet on the computer and explain to the children the information in the columns. Point out that we use a great deal of water and that over a week one person may use water in the following way:

A	B	C	D	E	F	G	H
1	Mon	Tues	Wed	Thur	Fri	Sat	Sun
2 Shower	25	25	25	25	25	25	25
3 Washing	10	10	10	10	10	10	10
4 Washing Machine	100	100	100	100	100	100	100
5 Cooking	10	10	10	10	10	10	10
6 Washing up	10	10	10	10	10	10	10
7 Toilet	10	10	10	10	10	10	10
8 Drinking	5	5	5	5	5	5	5
9 Total	175	175	175	175	175	175	175
10 Total for week			1225				

Explain to the children that each figure in the spreadsheet shows how many litres of water are used for each activity once during the day. For example, the toilet uses ten litres of water per flush so the toilet in our example is only used once in the day. Each day is shown exactly the same. On the spreadsheet cells B9, C9, D9, E9, F9, G9 and H9 show the daily totals and cell D10 shows the weekly total.

Invite the children to alter the spreadsheet by discussing how often the various uses of water will be applied each day and to put in the new figures. Ask them to write down the reasons for the changes. Suggest that they make some of the changes by estimating how often appliances are used each day. Alternatively, suggest that they carry out experiments and research to produce more accurate consumption figures than have been indicated. When the children have adapted their spreadsheet, give them the following task to solve: 'There is a serious drought and you have to cut the water consumption of the user to less than 800 litres per week (the figure could differ according to the children's spreadsheet).' Ask the children to alter the spreadsheet until consumption is less than 800 litres in a week. Explain that they must keep the figures in the spreadsheet sensible and that they must give reasons for the alterations. Let them use a tape recorder to record the discussions if they want to.

Follow-up

Introduce a cost for the water and ask the children to try to make the water bill as low as possible. They will need to include another two cells on the spreadsheet. One would hold the price of water per litre and the other would be the weekly total multiplied by the cell containing the price per litre. Tell them that another person is coming to stay. How much extra will the water cost for that person? Will twice as much water be used?

Space in a room

Age range

Eleven and over.

Group size

Small groups.

What you need

A computer system, a simple spreadsheet, chairs of various sizes, tape measures.

Starting points

Ask the children to imagine that they are going to sell tickets for a show in school and that they need to know how many seats they can fit into the hall. This will give them an idea of how many tickets to print and how much money they will make. Discuss the fact that they need to measure the area of the hall where chairs can be put and how much room each chair takes up, including leg and arm room for the audience. Should they put out smaller chairs for younger children and get more in? How will this affect the takings if the younger children pay less for their tickets?

What to do

Ask the children to collect three different sizes of chairs from around the school and measure the space each one needs, taking into account leg and arm room. Let them measure the area of the hall but make sure they allow room for a gangway and entrance, if necessary. Ask the children to decide on a price for each size of seat: adult, older child, younger child. Let them enter the figures into the spreadsheet along the following lines:

	A	B	C	D
1	No. size 1	No. size 2	No. size 3	
2	20	30	40	
3	Price (p)			
4	75	60	45	
5	Money taken	£51	Area (Depends on area of each chair.)	

The money taken (cell B5) will be cells A2 × A4 + B2 × B4 + C2 × C4 divided by 100 to give the total in pounds. The area (cell D5) will be cell A2 × area of size 1 chair + cell B2 × area of size 2 chair + cell C2 × area of size 3 chair. This total area must not be greater than the size of the available room.

Ask the children to alter the spreadsheet to solve various problems such as getting the maximum number of people in, making the most money and altering the charges so that by admitting younger children the profits are not affected.

Follow-up

Ask the children to solve the problem of maximising profits if children were allowed in at half price. Which chair size would produce the maximum profit?

Making a box

Age range

Eleven and over.

Group size

Small groups.

What you need

A computer system, a simple spreadsheet, rectangular pieces of cardboard.

Starting points

Show the children how they can make an open box from a rectangular piece of cardboard by cutting out equal-sized squares from each of the corners and folding up the ends. Discuss how to calculate the volume of the box.

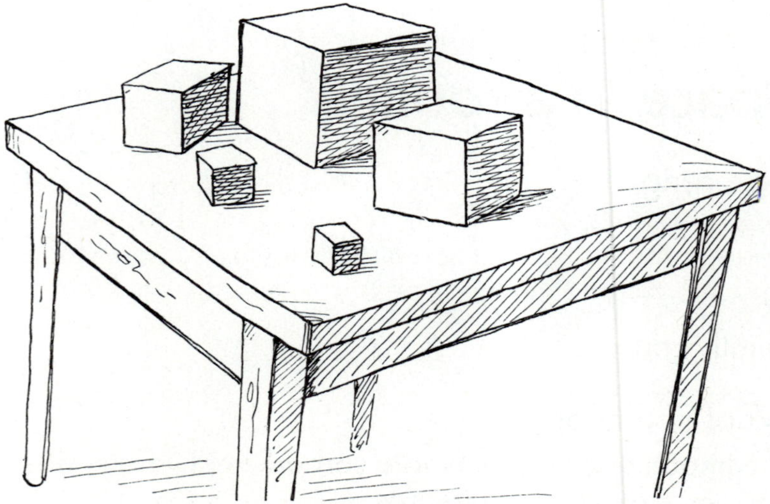

What to do

Explain to the children that they are to pretend that they run a factory that makes boxes. The factory must keep its costs as low as possible. Ask them to find the maximum volume of a box that can be made from a piece of cardboard 60cm long and 40cm wide. Let them use a spreadsheet such as the following, to help work out the problem.

	A	B	C	D
1	Size of square	2cm		
2	Length of card	60	Length of box	56
3	Width of card	40	Width of box	36
4			Height of box	2
5	Volume of box	4032		

Cell D2 contains the length of card minus twice the length of the square cut off (cell B2 − 2 × cell B1). Cell D3 contains the width of card minus twice the length of the square cut off (cell B3 − 2 × cell B1). The height of the box is a copy of cell C1 and the volume of the box in cell B5 is cells D2 × D3 × D4. Ask the children to change the number which gives the size of the square and the volume will change automatically.

When the children have solved the problem, ask them to find the largest volume if the box had a lid. To make it easier, ask them to visualise that the lid is the same size as the base of the box. Explain that when the squares have been cut off, the length of the card left has to be divided equally between the base and the lid.

Follow-up

For more able children, tell them that a company selling soap powder wants a box measuring 3000 cubic centimetres but they want to use as little card as possible to make the box. What size of card do they need to produce a box without a lid? Ask the children to experiment with the three number values – size of square, length and width of card. Tell them to alter only one at a time, to assess the effect of the change on the volume of the box. Suggest that they consider questions such as 'Is it better to have a tall or a square box?'

Journeys with your floor turtle

Floor turtling in the classroom is concerned with controlling a robot with the aid of a computer. This exciting activity supports the Measurement and Control Strand of Information Technology Capability in the National Curriculum. Two main types of floor turtle are in general use in classrooms today. One is the Jessop Turtle which resembles a Perspex dome on wheels and is connected to the computer by a long lead. The second is the Valiant Turtle which looks like a real turtle and is remotely controlled by the computer.

A robotic device such as a floor turtle introduces children to the use of the programming language LOGO. This is looked at in greater detail in the next chapter. Children's ability to manipulate a screen turtle effectively is made easier by first using a turtle on the floor. The computer is used in exactly the same way to control the movement of both a floor and a screen turtle. When children begin to control a floor turtle, you do not have to give them complex instructions and it is sensible

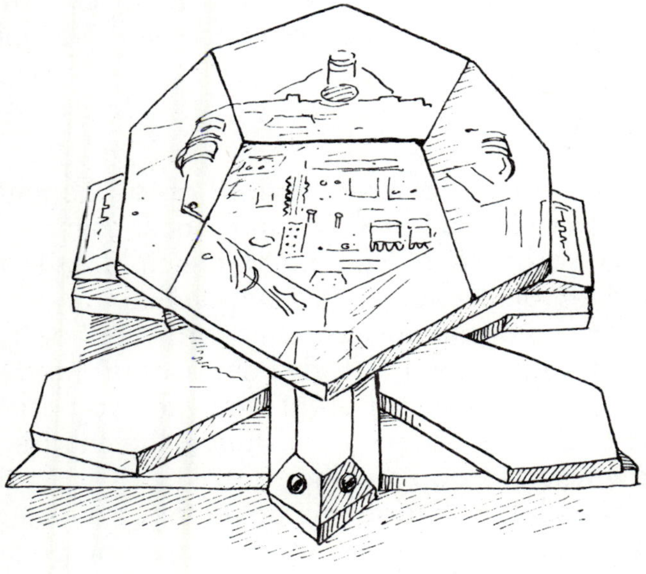

to set up the turtle so that only one press of a computer key is needed for any one movement of the turtle. This is possible whichever version of LOGO you have.

In all the chapter's suggested activities for using a floor turtle, the driving of the turtle can be done at the child's level. This may mean setting up a one-key-press program, it could mean using the commands of LOGO or it could, later on, mean the writing of LOGO procedures to make the turtle move. These three levels of using LOGO form a progression which the children work through as they gain more experience of using the LOGO language.

The activities in the chapter not only integrate other areas of the curriculum but also cross curriculum boundaries. You will be able to identify many curriculum areas within each activity and, in addition, there are various skills that will be used and used again as the children carry out the ideas. These include:

- moving and turning;
- listening and responding;
- sequencing and estimating;
- designing and planning;
- evaluating and modifying.

A floor turtle can make only four movements: it can travel either forwards or backwards and it can turn on the spot, either to the left or to the right. The children can use any combination or sequence containing these four commands to move the turtle to a given destination. The controlling of an inanimate object such as a floor turtle can be very difficult for early years children unless they have moved in the same way. The introduction of the floor turtle will be made a lot smoother if you make the movements familiar to the children and give them the opportunity to take on the role of a robotic device for themselves. The first two activities in the chapter have been devised for this purpose.

Once the children are familiar with the movements of a robot and are able to respond to robot commands for themselves, they will be ready to control a device such as a floor turtle from the computer.

From the third activity onwards, you will need a computer with LOGO or its equivalent, a floor turtle and floor space in which a floor turtle can move.

Many of the floor turtle activities involve children in creating resources to use with the floor turtle or preparing and planning the time they spend operating the floor turtle. This means that although they may not be working directly with the computer, they will be carrying out work and activities associated with the computer, thus reducing the pressure on computer time.

All the activities in the chapter have a floor turtle; however, most of them could be carried out with an independent floor-crawling robot such as Roamer or Pip.

Note

For details of the floor turtles and other robotic devices, refer to the Resources pages at the back of this book.

Learning to move

Age range
Five to seven.

Group size
The whole class or small groups.

What you need
A large floor area, wrist bands for each child to indicate left and right.

Starting points
Discuss with the children what they think it would be like to be a robot. Remind them that robots do not 'know' anything. Explain that they are programmed to do certain things and only respond to given commands. Discuss with them what is meant by moving forward and back and which direction is which. Also, discuss the difference between left and right and see if the children know the difference.

What to do
Space the children out over the floor area. 'Command' the children to move 'forward' and 'back' using only these two words. Next, 'command' the children to turn right and left on the spot, without travelling any distance; once again only use the words 'left' or 'right'. The wrist bands come in handy here as a prompt.

It will soon become apparent that when you ask them to move and do not specify a distance, the children will not know when to stop moving.

Discuss with the children the advantages of using a standard distance of movement, perhaps one pace, for

forward and back and show them how to move in quarter turns for both left and right.

Now give them an instruction of 'forward one' or 'back two'. The children's pace will differ, of course, but they will be able to complete a command or set of commands and come to a stop, thereby not requiring 'stop' to be given as a command.

Turning is more difficult; not only do children have to carry out an instruction of a quarter turn to the right or left but they also have to decide which is their left and right. This can be very confusing. A turn of right four or left four would be a complete turn on the spot, while a turn of right two would be a turn through 180° and a turn of left one would be a turn of 90° to the left.

With practice, the children will know how to move and how far to move, as a number or unit of measure will have been identified and introduced.

To begin with, children will only listen to and respond to one instruction at a time. You can gradually build this up so that they will listen to and remember two, then three, then four instructions before responding.

Follow-up

- Use a 'Simon says' approach as you give commands.
- Allow the children to work in pairs, one being the 'robot', the other giving the instructions.
- Allow the children to work in groups so that one instructor has many 'robots' to control. In this activity, give the 'robots' numbers so that only the 'robot' asked responds to the instructions. Let the children carry out these activities in a PE session or in the playground.

Finding the spot

Age range

Five to seven.

Group size

Pairs.

What you need

A large floor area, an identified destination point.

Starting points

Discuss with the children what we do to reach certain places. Suggest that we could ask someone who has already been somewhere to give us the instructions on how to get there. Point out the need to listen very carefully to instructions before acting on them.

What to do

Explain to the children that, for this activity, one person in each pair will take the role of a robot, while the other will be the instructor giving the instructions to the robot.

Point out that the robot should stand still on a defined spot and that its destination, some distance away, has to be identified by the instructor. The aim of the activity is for the instructor to make the robot reach the destination point. The children must do this by giving the correct sequence of instructions using a combination of the four commands listed in the previous activity. Ensure that the children give precise instructions so that the robot reaches the destination point.

Follow-up

Encourage the children to record the instructions they give. This will become the route to the destination so that the robot can travel it again. Point out the importance of remembering the exact starting point of the robot and the direction faced; otherwise they may find it difficult to retrace the route.

Home for a turtle

Age range

Five to seven.

Group size

Small groups.

What you need

Cardboard boxes, paper, cardboard tubes, tissue paper, paints, crayons, adhesive, sticky tape, a computer loaded with LOGO or its equivalent, a floor turtle.

Starting points

Discuss with the children where we live and what we live in. Ask them to consider the amenities we enjoy and have around us, such as friends' houses to visit, shops to buy food, parks and play areas to play in.

What to do

Tell the children that their 'turtle' should also have a home. From the materials available, let the children design and make a house for their turtle to live in and a garden to surround it. Once the house and garden are made, let the children move the turtle around its new environment and explore what is there.

Make sure the children know how to command the turtle to move and ensure that they keep the commands simple.

This activity allows you to use prepositions which you can introduce to the children. 'Move the turtle to the house', 'Go by the flowers', 'Go into the house', 'Go to the back of the house' and so on.

Amazing turtle

Age range
Five to seven.

Group size
Pairs or small groups.

What you need
Skittles or building bricks or boxes, a computer loaded with LOGO or an equivalent language, a floor turtle.

Starting points
Discuss the type of maze puzzle that the children might have played in activity books. Talk about how their turtle might find his way through a maze.

What to do
Show the children how they can use the skittles, building blocks or boxes to build a maze for their turtle to move through. Let them design and build their own maze and, using the computer, move the turtle from start to finish.

Follow-up
Suggest to the children that they introduce friends for their turtle and make homes for them so the turtle can visit them. Let them build a playground area with swings and roundabouts for the turtle to relax in. Ask them to create an environment that takes account of a humanities project which you are currently working on. Let the children experiment with using scrap materials to decorate the turtle and turn it into different animals or characters.

Use the computer time well by allowing one pair or group to use the computer while the other groups plan their maze. Ask the children if they can predict the instructions they will have to give to the turtle.

Follow-up

- Make sure the computer operator cannot see the turtle in the maze and can only be guided by the instructions of another child.
- Encourage the children to record the instructions needed to direct the turtle through the maze. This will become the route plan for that maze. See if the children can rebuild their maze and travel through it using the previously recorded instructions.

Tenpin turtle

Age range

Five to seven.

Group size

Pairs or small groups.

What you need

Ten skittles, a computer loaded with LOGO or an equivalent, a floor turtle.

Starting points

Ask the children if any of them has ever been to a tenpin bowling alley. Talk about the children's experiences there, or describe to them what happens there. Discuss the setting up of the skittles. Let the children practise counting and number bonds to ten.

What to do

Show the children how to set up the skittles and tell them to drive the turtle towards them to knock down as many skittles as possible. Ask them to count how many skittles were knocked over with their first push and how many skittles are still standing.

Let another child move the turtle to knock down more skittles. Ask them to continue to count how many skittles fall at each move and how many moves it takes to knock all the skittles down.

While one group is using the computer, ask the other children to consider how to make the turtle more efficient at knocking down the skittles.

Follow-up

- Invite the children to record on paper how many skittles they knocked over at each move and how many were still standing. Let them also record how many moves it takes to knock them all down.
- Encourage the children to find a way of knocking down the skittles more efficiently. Suggest that they add an arm to the turtle.
- Set up varying numbers of skittles so that the children can practise other number bonds.

Transporting turtle

Age range
Six to seven.

Group size
Small groups.

What you need
Boxes, paints, coloured paper, adhesive, string, writing paper, pencils, crayons, sticky tape, a computer loaded with LOGO or an equivalent, a floor turtle.

Starting points
Discuss with the children the idea that communication between people is very important, especially if they cannot talk directly to each other. To set the activity in context, let the children write messages for someone else in the class. Ask, 'If we can't talk, how might the turtle help us to get messages to one another?'

What to do
Using the boxes, paper and paints, ask the children to transform the turtle into a vehicle. Suggest that they use string to attach a carrying container which the turtle can pull. Ask the children to put a written message into the container and move the turtle to the person who should receive the message.

While one group works at the computer, ask the other groups to write their messages for delivery, or to design their container and work out how to attach it to the turtle.

Follow-up

- Let the children try to get the turtle to deliver a written message to another class or class area.
- Ask the children to use the turtle to carry lightweight objects between people or places.
- Let the children use the turtle and the carrier in other contexts, for example, collecting litter.

Magnetic turtle

Age range
Five to seven.

Group size
Small groups.

What you need
Magnets, string, metal objects (some magnetic, others not), a computer loaded with LOGO or an equivalent, a floor turtle.

Starting points
Discuss with the children how magnets attract and repel. Talk with them about the need to recycle aluminium. Discuss the fact that aluminium is not attracted to magnets and how it can be sorted out from other metals. Let the children investigate the metal objects to find out which are magnetic and which are not.

What to do
Suggest to the children that they make the turtle into a moving magnet by attaching a number of magnets to it with string. Using the computer, let the children move the turtle among magnetic and non-magnetic metal objects and pick up the magnetic ones. As one group works at the computer, ask the other groups to consider which metal objects to lay on the floor.

Follow-up
- Let the children use the magnetic turtle to distinguish between steel and aluminium cans for recycling purposes.

- Ask the children to pretend that the magnetic turtle is a metal detector looking for coins at a Roman site.
- Let the children use the magnetic turtle as a detector for buried treasure.

Route-marching turtle

Age range
Six to eight.

Group size
Pairs or small groups.

What you need
Squared paper, large sheets of paper, pencils, Blu-Tack, a computer loaded with LOGO or an equivalent, a floor turtle.

Starting points
Discuss with the children what we need to do before we set off on a journey to make sure we arrive at the right place and at the right time. Emphasise that the route must be planned. Talk with the children about preparing a route for the turtle to take. Squared paper will help give the route a scale or number of moves needed to move the turtle.

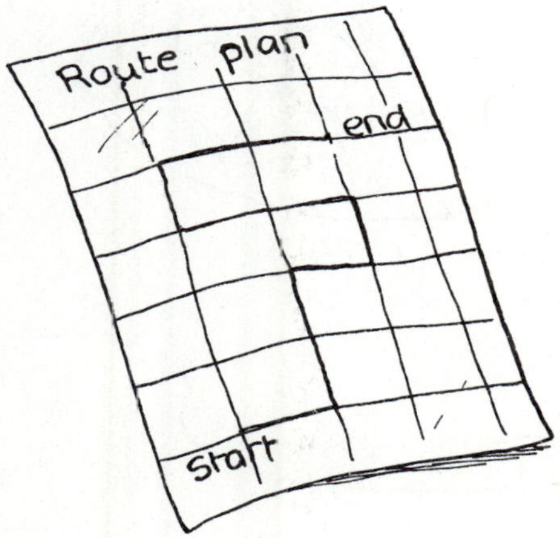

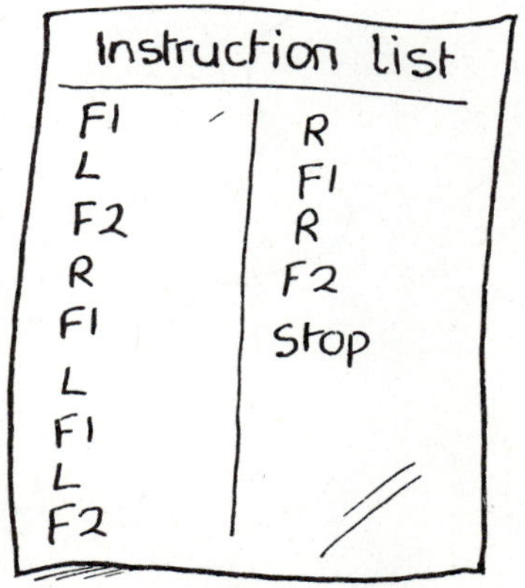

What to do
Using the squared paper, show the children how to plan a route to a given destination. Let each square be equivalent to one turtle move. Let the children plan and draw their own route on squared paper; they can then use this as the route for the turtle to take. Explain how to translate the plan into a list of commands that the turtle will need to follow the route on the floor.

Using the large pieces of paper, let the children mark their route plan on the floor. Invite the children to make the turtle follow the list of instructions from their route plans. They will soon see whether or not their list of commands is correct for their route. If the commands are not correct, ask them to modify the instruction list, not the route plan.

Follow-up

- Let one group of children follow the route with the turtle and let a second group make the return journey. On the return journey, the turtle could move either forwards or backwards. Ask the children to record the route of the return journey.
- Encourage the children to lay out on the floor another route for the turtle to take. Ask them to write down the commands they think will take the turtle along the route. Let them use their commands to see if the turtle can successfully travel the route. If it cannot, ask them to alter the instruction list to complete the route successfully.
- If the children are at the stage of using LOGO to control the turtle, show them how to write a LOGO procedure from the instruction list they already have. Ask them to save it on the disk and let them load and use the procedure in another session.

Turtle trails

Age range
Five to seven.

Group size
Small groups.

What you need
A turtle pen, a floor area you can write on or large sheets of paper, a computer loaded with LOGO or an equivalent, a floor turtle.

Starting points
Talk with the children about how they have learned to move the turtle and that it can travel wherever they wish.

Talk about how they have recorded its movements. Explain that the turtle can hold a pen at its centre point and that the pen allows the turtle to draw its own route plan of where it has been. Discuss when it would be an advantage for the turtle to draw its own trail and when it would not be.

What to do

Select a floor area that can be drawn on or ask the children to spread paper out on the floor. Insert a turtle pen into the floor turtle. Using the computer, let the children experiment with the drawing turtle to see what they can create. While one group uses the computer, ask the other groups to plan a route for the turtle to take.

Follow-up

- Let the children use the drawing turtle to draw regular shapes.
- Ask the children to use the turtle to draw something specific, such as a house. Explain to them that they may sometimes need to pull the pen up so that it does not draw wherever it goes. Let the children enhance or complete the drawings away from the turtle.

Learning with LOGO

LOGO is a computer language easy enough for young children to use but powerful enough to stretch adults. Seymour Papert, the main architect of the language, saw it as an environment where children are allowed to explore and discover for themselves with as little help as possible from the teacher. In fact, the teacher's role was just to introduce the language as and when necessary. The idea of teacher-given tasks or worksheets is very much contrary to the way Papert says LOGO should be used by children.

This approach can work but only where LOGO has a place in the curriculum in all classes, no matter what age. One teacher in year five or six cannot hope to achieve success with LOGO unless it has been used in all the previous years. This rarely happens at the present time, so it is for this reason that some tasks need to be introduced to the children which will help to put this right and encourage the reluctant teacher to try LOGO.

The ideas in this chapter can be slotted in where necessary and should help to focus on the mathematical skills required or parts of the language needed at various times. Although age ranges are suggested, they very much depend on the experience of the child.

The order in which you introduce the LOGO commands to the children will depend on their ability and when they need them for a project that they have chosen. However, the basic order should be as follows:

1. Instant-action mode with FORWARD, BACK, RIGHT and LEFT. This means that typing in FORWARD 100 will immediately cause the turtle to move forward by 100 units. The PENUP and PENDOWN commands can also be introduced. In this mode, the commands will not be remembered by the computer and cannot be saved.

2. Procedure mode. This means that the computer is taught a new word or command. For example, the computer is taught the word SQUARE and is given the instructions REPEAT 4 [FORWARD 100 RIGHT 90]. This is called a procedure and when the name of the procedure is typed in, as in SQUARE, the instructions are carried out and a square is drawn. When the name is typed in, we say we have 'called' the procedure. Because the computer has been taught the word SQUARE, another procedure can be built that will use the word SQUARE in its instructions. In such a case, we say that one procedure has 'called' another.

3. Introduction of variables. If the procedure SQUARE had a variable instead of the length of forward movement, then it would be possible to draw a square of any size. This makes the procedure very powerful and flexible.

You can introduce many of the other commands but the above procedures form the basis of good LOGO programming.

Hit the target

Age range
Seven to eight.

Group size
Pairs.

What you need
A computer system fitted with LOGO or a simple turtle program.

Starting points
If possible, introduce the children to the screen turtle while they are involved with the floor turtle so that the two can be seen moving together. Refer to the slowness of the floor turtle and why, for that reason, it might be an idea to use the screen turtle on its own.

What to do
Encourage the children to make precise movements with a screen turtle. Use the screen turtle to draw two small circles, one on each side of the screen. Then send the turtle to the middle of the screen. Set the screen to 'WRAP' so that the turtle will not disappear off the screen altogether. Make the instructions into a procedure so that it can be used as often as necessary.

Allocate each child in the pair one of the circles and tell them to take it in turns to input an angle followed by a distance to try and get the turtle inside the target. Make the task into a game; the first child to get the whole of the turtle into the circle is the winner. This will give the children practice in estimating distance and angles as each time one child fails to reach the target, the other has a different starting point with the turtle facing the opposite direction.

Follow-up
Encourage the children to attempt to draw shapes on the screen ready for small LOGO projects.

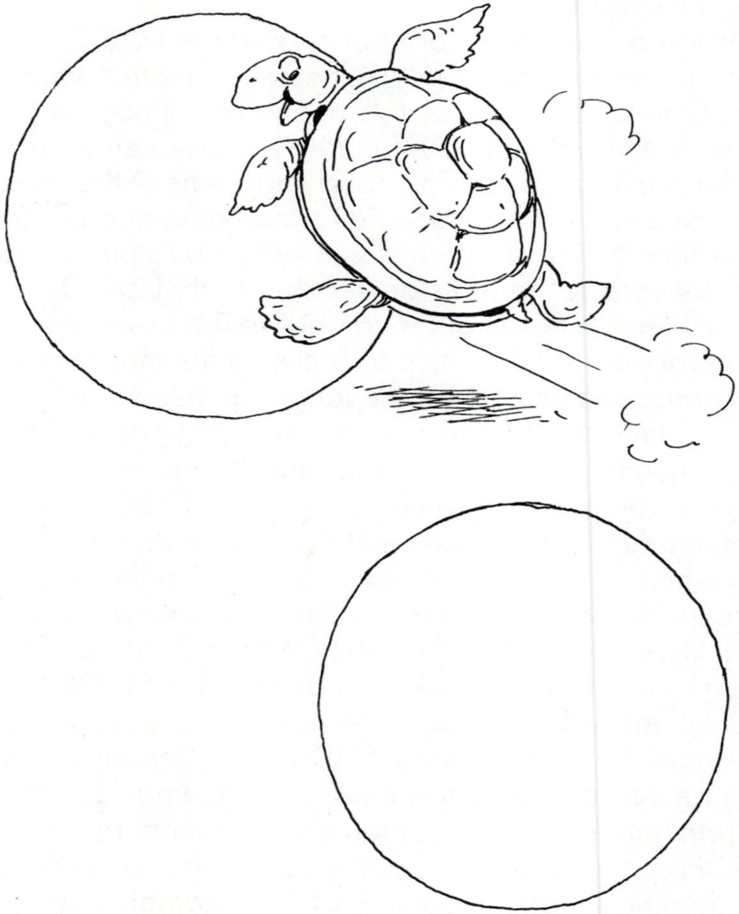

Draw a square

Age range
Seven to eight.

Group size
Pairs.

What you need
A computer system fitted with LOGO.

Starting points
Following an initial period of moving the turtle around, encourage the children to talk about the possibility of drawing something with the turtle. They will probably suggest a square or a picture that would contain a square. Since the square and the oblong are used as the basis for many LOGO drawings, it is important that the children can construct them easily.

What to do
Ask the children to draw a square using LOGO. They may need your help when choosing the number for the turn but encourage them to experiment. If necessary, invite them to act the part of the turtle themselves and walk the shape, making sure they return to the original position.

When they have discovered the method of drawing the square, ask them to draw smaller and bigger squares in different parts of the screen. Introduce PENUP and PENDOWN commands at this stage. Ask the children to find out what happens if they draw several squares which start in the same place but get bigger each time.

Follow-up
With the children, discuss the similarity of the FORWARD and TURN commands when drawing a square. The fact that the same command is repeated four times can be used to introduce the REPEAT command. This should lead on to the fact that the turtle returns to its original position and has actually turned through 360°. This can introduce the drawing of other shapes, encouraging the children to discover that

$$\frac{360}{\text{the number of sides}} = \text{the angle of turn}$$

Building a procedure

Age range
Eight to nine.

Group size
Pairs.

What you need
A computer system fitted with LOGO, a pencil, paper.

Starting points
Ask the children to control another child pretending to be a turtle walking a square. Tell them to use a number of paces for the forward movement. Explain that the next time they should not tell the 'turtle' each instruction but should just say, 'square'. Explain that the turtle has been taught to draw a square and should be able to do it every time they ask.

You can also use this exercise to introduce the idea of a variable for later work. Tell the children that when they say, 'square', they must follow it with a number and then the 'turtle' will walk a square the size of that number of paces.

What to do
Using the pencil and paper, go through with the children how the turtle draws a square, writing down each instruction. Children who have been introduced to the REPEAT command will be able to use this. Explain that if the children entered these instructions into the computer, the turtle would respond right away. Point out that, to teach the computer, they have to put the instructions into a procedure. Ask them to write on their paper at the beginning of their instructions TO SQUARE or BUILD SQUARE, depending on the type of LOGO you have. Following the instructions, ask the children to write the word END. Emphasise the importance of the two statements.

Tell the children to enter their instructions into the computer, noting that the turtle does not respond. Ask them to enter the word SQUARE and the turtle will respond, showing that it has 'learned' the word SQUARE. Ask the children to try moving the turtle several times calling SQUARE after every move. Let them then turn the turtle several times calling SQUARE after each turn. Ask them to combine a small movement and a small turn before calling SQUARE and the children will soon come up with a variety of patterns.

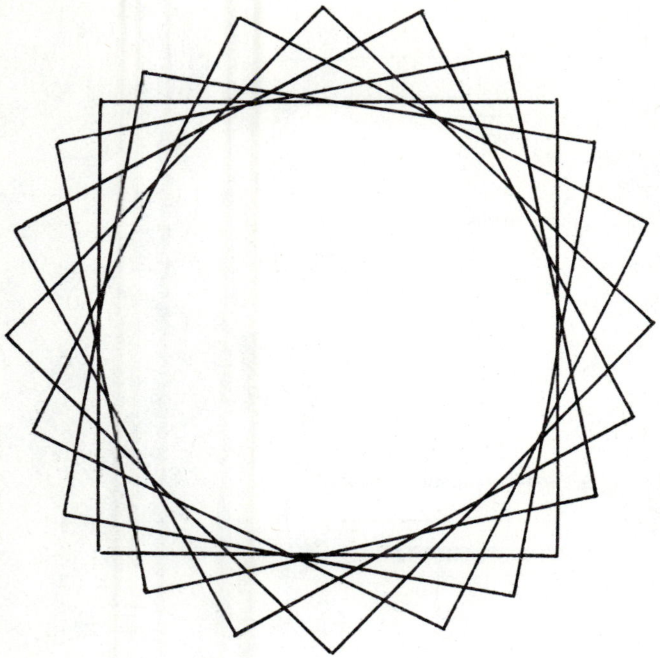

Shape up

Age range
Eight to nine.

Group size
Pairs.

What you need
A computer system fitted with LOGO, a collection of procedures produced in the previous activity.

Starting points
Talk to the children about the way shapes are made up of repeated instructions. Ask them what would happen if they called a procedure, moved the turtle in some way, called the procedure again and continued to do the same.

Follow-up
Let the children write procedures for other shapes. Introduce 'the editor' for changing a procedure if it does not work as expected. The editor is a separate screen or a screen window which allows you to change existing procedures. You can write new procedures from within the editor. Encourage the children to write a procedure which calls another, such as SQUARE. For example, a new procedure called PATTERN could have the instructions, REPEAT 6 [SQUARE RIGHT 30]. On entering or calling the procedure PATTERN, the turtle would draw a square and turn right 30° and it would do this six times. You could also introduce the children to saving procedures at this stage.

What to do

Ask the children to experiment by drawing a square (calling the procedure SQUARE), turning or moving the turtle a little and calling SQUARE again. Encourage them to build a procedure where they can repeat several times calling of SQUARE and turning a little.

Once they have grasped this idea, ask them to combine two shapes. This can be done in a variety of ways but the main ones are:

- Call a procedure to draw a shape, turn a little and call a procedure to draw a different shape. This will produce a circular pattern.
- Include one procedure in another. For example, in a procedure to draw a hexagon, each time the turtle moves forward a distance, follow it by a procedure to draw a square whose side is the same length as the side of a hexagon.

Follow-up

- Ask the children to find combinations of shapes that fit together or tesselate.
- Encourage them to begin using combinations of their procedures to produce pictures for topics they are working on in class.

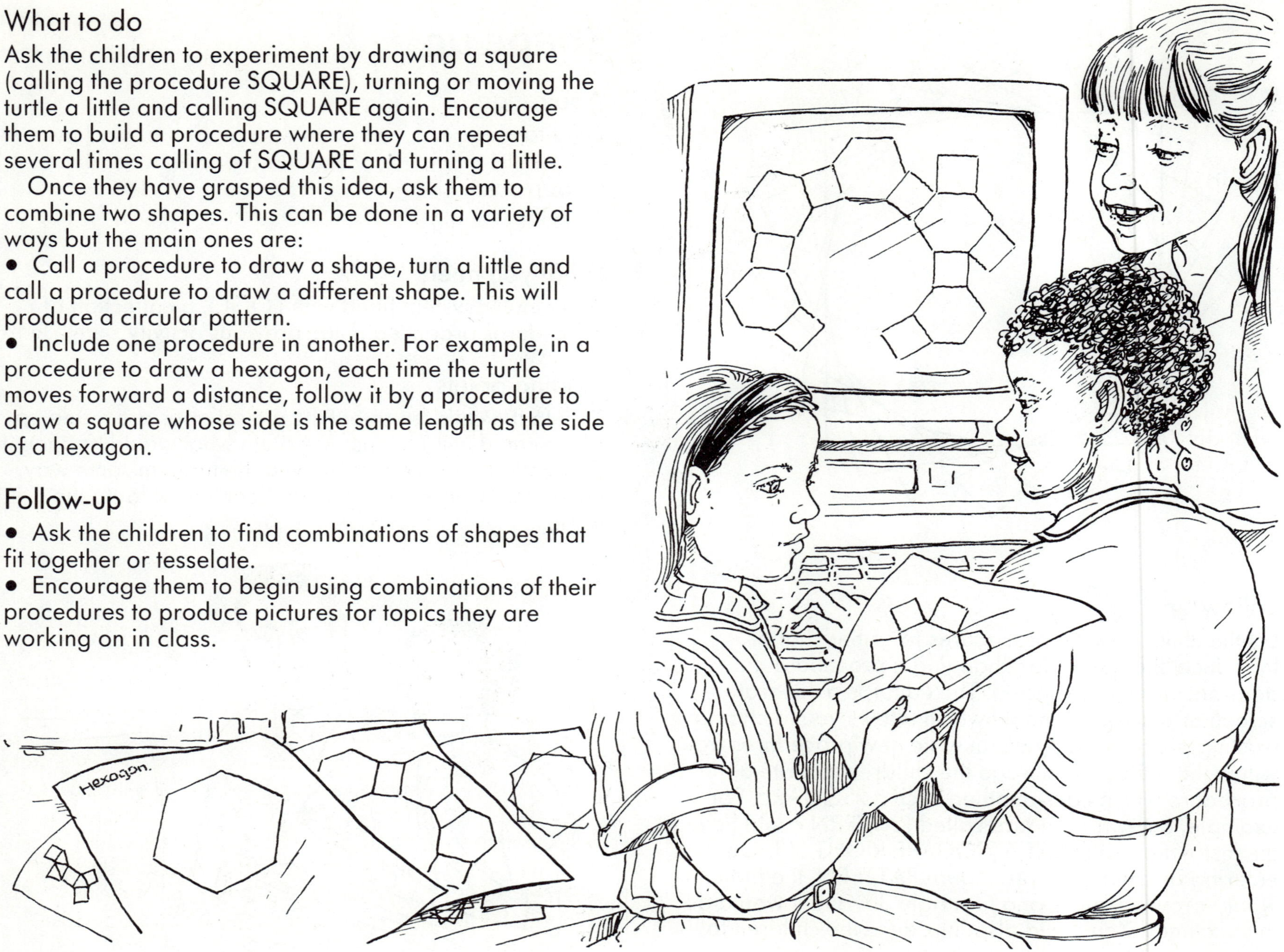

LOGO time

Age range
Nine to eleven.

Group size
Pairs or small groups.

What you need
A computer system fitted with LOGO, a stop-watch.

Starting points
Ask the children to observe the movement of hands of an analogue clock. How do the hands move – smoothly or jerkily? Explain to them that they are going to use LOGO to model the way clock hands move.

What to do
Explain to the children that the project is to design a clock where the time passes in seconds, that is, a clock with only a second hand.

In a discussion, encourage the children to say how they would draw the second hand. FORWARD plus a number should do the trick. Then go on to decide how to draw it at its next position. The procedure is in fact very simple:

FORWARD 200 (This will draw a line 200 units long.)

WAIT A MOMENT (This will be tested so that a new line will be drawn every second.)

CHANGE TURTLE PEN TO ERASE

BACK 200 (The line will disappear.)

RIGHT 6 DEGREES (60 seconds will take the turtle round 360°.)

SET THE PEN TO DRAW AGAIN

GO BACK TO THE FORWARD 200

Encourage the children to make the instructions into a procedure and if that procedure calls itself, the whole process becomes continuous. This idea of the procedure calling itself is called recursion and is a very powerful part of LOGO. For example, in this procedure which we could call TICK, the last instruction would be TICK which would start the whole process again until we stopped it.

Ask the children to check the precision of the timer. The part that says WAIT should be adjusted until it is accurate over a minute. Let the children use a stop-watch to check this. Where LOGO can use simple sound, ask the children to find a way of producing a ticking noise.

Follow-up

If the children find the activity relatively straightforward, introduce the idea of a complete working clock. The second hand moves 60 times (one minute) and the minute hand moves once (an angle of 6°). Every time the minute hand moves ten times, the hour hand moves once (6°). You could refine this even further so the minute hand and the hour hand move in smaller amounts. Show the children how numbers could be put on the clock. Could they produce a clock that tells the right time?

Digital numbers

Age range

Nine to eleven.

Group size

Pairs or small groups.

What you need

A computer system fitted with LOGO, a clock with digital display (or any device that shows numbers as a series of lights), paper, coloured pencils.

Starting points

Ask the children if any of them have a watch. You will probably discover two basic types of display, analogue and digital. Ask the children how the two types differ. At the end of the discussion, make sure that they realise that in a digital display different numbers appear in the same place.

What to do

With the help of the digital display clock, show the children how the numbers 0 to 9 can be presented by a series of lines being highlighted in a digital display. Ask them to count them so that they can see that most of these types of device work on a seven-line display. Let the children draw all the numbers on paper using the seven lines. Give the children a sheet of seven line displays and ask them to draw over them using a coloured pencil.)

Ask each group of children to get the turtle to draw one of the numbers. Advise them to use only forward movements and 90° angles, using PENUP and PENDOWN commands to move over unlit areas.

Follow-up

When the children have created a number, ask them to try using the procedure they have produced to write the number twice, side by side. This may lead to problems, so encourage them to start always at the same point, follow the same route round the seven lines and only use PENUP and PENDOWN to make the marks. A final movement at the end will put the turtle in a position ready to draw the next number. Introduce more difficulties, depending on the ability of the children. For example, you could ask them to make the procedures draw numbers of different sizes in the same way.

Jumping turtle

Age range

Eight to ten.

Group size

Pairs or small groups.

What you need

A computer system fitted with LOGO, graph paper, pencils.

Starting points

Give each child a piece of graph paper and ask them to draw *x* and *y* axes on it. (The position and number values of the axes will depend on the screen mode used by the computer.) Let the children draw a simple straight line shape on the graph paper. Discourage them from drawing a rectangle.

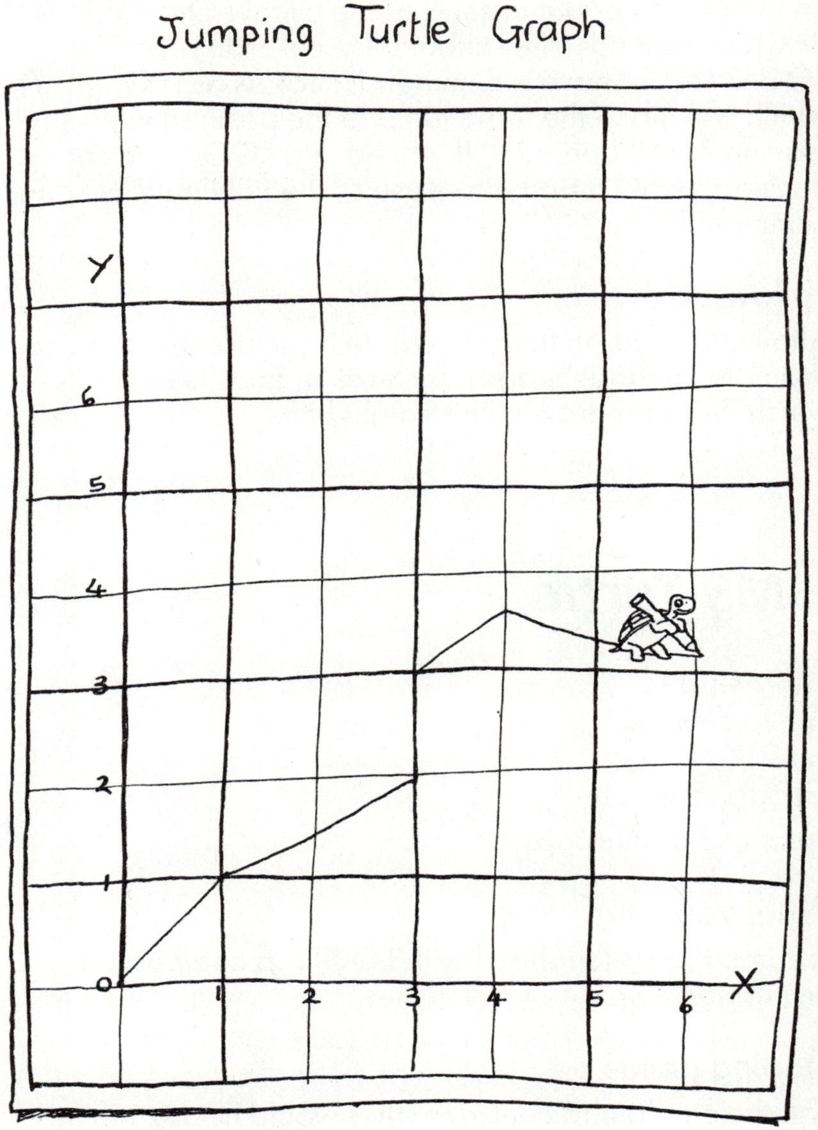

What to do

Ask the children to draw the same shape using the turtle on the computer but instead of the usual FORWARD and BACK commands, they should use co-ordinates. The LOGO should have a command, such as SETPOS (X, Y), which will make the turtle jump to the position *x, y* leaving a trail behind it. If you have a LOGO which does not leave a trail make use of the PENDOWN command.

Follow-up

Allow the children to try to create a picture using the co-ordinate method. Suggest pictures of houses or boats which they can draw with straight lines.

HMS *Turtle*

Age range

Ten to eleven.

Group size

Pairs or small groups.

What you need

A computer system fitted with LOGO, a compass, a protractor.

Starting points

Ask the children to consider what would happen if the turtle were a ship. Would the captain tell it to go forward, backward, right and left? Ask the children what commands the captain might give if he were following a map or chart.

What to do

Ask the children to imagine that the turtle is a ship on the ocean. Explain to them that the turtle does not know how to go north, south, east or west but it can be told to face a certain direction based on headings. For example, east is 90°. The computer will respond to a command such as SETH 90, which will make the turtle face to the right of the screen. We can use this command to teach the turtle how to go north, south, east, west and so on.

Tell the children that they must teach the turtle to travel in the direction that they request. For example, if they say NORTH 50 the turtle will go towards the top of the screen a distance of 50 units. Ask them to write procedures for 4, 8 or 16 points of the compass, depending on their ability. A possible procedure for south could be:

```
TO SOUTH :distance
SETH 180
FD :distance
END
```

If the children have had little or no experience of variables in procedures, this is an ideal exercise for introducing them. By following SOUTH with a variable, in this case :distance, the forward movement (FD) in the procedure can be left as a variable, as shown. When SOUTH is written, LOGO expects a number to follow which will be used by the FORWARD (FD) command.

Any shape, any size

Age range
Ten to eleven.

Group size
Pairs or small groups.

What you need
A computer system fitted with LOGO.

Starting points
Children involved in this activity should have had some experience of drawing simple shapes and be able to use variables in their procedures. Discuss with them how to draw a square by repeating four times a forward movement and right or left 90°. Talk about other shapes, how many times the procedure needs to be repeated and what the angle will be. Suggest that they should have one procedure to draw all the shapes they need.

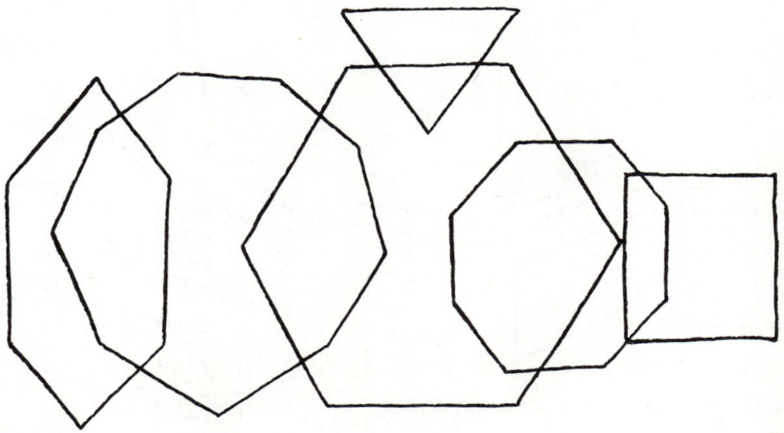

Follow-up
Tell the children to draw a simple map on the screen and choose a spot where they might find a buried treasure. Explain that they must 'sail' right round the island and then reach the buried treasure, using only the compass bearings that they have taught the turtle.

What to do

Explain to the children how to write a LOGO procedure for a shape which is called with a variable, the variable being the number of sides required. For example, if you call your procedure SHAPE, then you should be able to write SHAPE 6 and produce a hexagon or with SHAPE 3 produce a triangle. The procedure will then repeat, that number of times, a forward movement followed by an angle. The angle will depend on the number of sides but you can remind the children that when a shape has been completed, the turtle will have turned through 360°. In one version of LOGO, the procedure might look like this:

```
TO SHAPE :sides
REPEAT :sides [FD 100 RT 360/:sides]
END
```

Writing SHAPE 5 would repeat five times , and FORWARD 100 RIGHT 72 would produce a pentagon.

Follow-up

Introduce a second variable which is the length of forward movement. Once the children have grasped this concept, they will be able to draw shapes of any size and with any number of sides. Let the children experiment with these shapes. Ask them if it is possible to draw a circle using their procedure.

Fireworks

Age range
Nine to ten.

Group size
Pairs.

What you need
A computer system fitted with LOGO.

Starting points
Discuss with the children what happens to the screen turtle if they repeat something several times but make the forward movement or the angle increase or decrease each time. Let them try this in the playground with forward a pace, right 90, forward two paces and so on. Ask them what we call this type of shape. This introduction to spirals can then be tried on the computer.

What to do
Invite the children to make patterns like fireworks on the screen. Remind the children how to put a variable into a procedure and call the procedure SPIRAL :variable. Explain that all they need to do is complete a statement such as, FORWARD :variable RIGHT 90. The procedure then calls itself but adds one on to the variable, for instance, SPIRAL :variable+1. The procedure is thus recursive. If the children want to stop the procedure, they must enter a counting statement. This will allow them to put spirals at different points on the screen.

Introduce the colour options at this point to produce spirals of different colours. Invite the children to combine the SPIRAL procedure with the colour option to make the screen look like a firework display.

Follow-up
- Ask the children to try replacing 90 with the variable and keep the forward movement the same. For example, FORWARD 100 RIGHT :angle. Angle then becomes :angle+1 and so on.
- Let more able children try having two variables, one for the movement and one for the angle of turn.

Taking control

The idea of using technology to control devices or the general environment is fairly common in our society. There are two main types of control technology, manual and automatic.

Under manual control, a command has to be given directly to make something happen. A good example of this is the normal lighting system of a house; as it gets dark, you use a switch to turn on the light.

Many systems operate automatically. Very often, automatic systems need some form of sensor to send information to a system of switches to make devices turn on or off. A modern central heating system is a good example of this type of control. There is usually a timing mechanism so that when a certain time is reached, the whole or part of the system switches on or off. The temperature of the water flowing through the system is controlled by a thermostat which prevents the water in the boiler overheating. Another thermostat may measure the temperature in a room and switch radiators on and off to maintain a comfortable environment. The whole system depends on a series of sensors which automatically turn devices on and off.

A discussion of most households will uncover lots of examples of control technology – the washing machine, cooker, heating system, immersion heater, video recorder; the list is almost endless. Out and about, children experience control technology all the time and hardly realise it. Ask them how traffic lights work and how a pelican crossing near the school differs from the main lights at the crossroads in the centre of town. There is much to be gained from discussion as children will begin to understand how widespread and important control technology is. This, in turn, should stimulate their enthusiasm to see how and why they can set up control systems in the classroom.

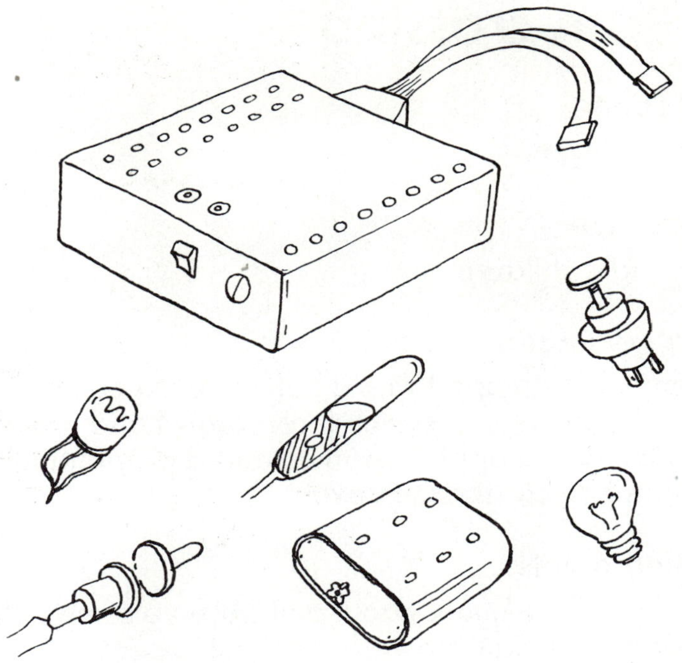

Firstly, you will need a buffer box which is simply an electronic device that attaches to your computer and allows you to attach switches which can input information into or send information out of the computer. You will also need some associated control software which will allow you to set up instructions to control the buffer box and everything attached to it. Lastly, you will need materials which allow children to make up models which they can control. This equipment could be commercially made such as Lego Technic or could consist of simple woodworking or craft resources.

The activities in this chapter are mostly relevant for children at the older end of the junior school. Younger children can make a useful start to control technology by using the floor turtle and floor-crawling robots such as Roamer and Pip.

Pelican crossing

Age range
Nine to eleven.

Group size
Six to eight children.

What you need
A computer equipped with a buffer box, a control software package, a switch (preferably hand press), bulbs (coloured or plain with coloured cellophane), wiring, small cardboard boxes.

Starting points
With the children, talk about and observe some pelican crossings in action. How are the lights operated? Discuss the reasons why they work as they do. The lights only need to operate when someone wants to cross the road; they do not need to be activated on an automatic sequence but they do need to follow a pattern once operated, so that the traffic is not held up for long periods of time.

Explain to the children that the buffer box has a series of inputs and outputs. The inputs allow switches and sensors to send messages to the computer. The outputs allow the computer to control external items such as lights, buzzers or motors.

What to do
Encourage the children to make a model of the lights at a pedestrian crossing. Explain that it will be operated via the computer. Ask the children to make up their set of lights. Let them wire up the bulbs in a small box with

cut-out holes covered with coloured cellophane. Explain that the bulb should be on green until the hand switch is pressed, when it should change to amber and then red. Tell them to wire the switch to input 1 on the buffer box. Explain that the green light could be on output 1 with the other lights on outputs 2 and 3. Tell them, in simple terms, how the system operates: when input 1 is off, output 1 is on. When input 1 is on, then output 2 comes on and waits for a short while; output 3 comes on and waits for a longer period of time. The children could set the times and sequences of the lights after observing real pelican crossing.

Follow-up
- Invite the children to integrate warning lights for pedestrians into the system.
- Ask them to integrate a flashing amber light into the system.

Traffic lights

Age range
Nine to eleven.

Group size
Six to eight children.

What you need
A computer with a buffer box, a control software package, bulbs, coloured cellophane, small boxes, dowelling, wiring.

Starting points
Talk with the children about the way traffic lights work. If possible, take the children out and let them observe traffic lights for a short time. Can the children see how different they are to pedestrian crossings? Do they know what these lights are designed to do? Explain that their main function is to control traffic flow at busy junctions and also to reduce the risk of accidents. They operate automatically, whereas pelican crossing lights react to the press of a button.

What to do
Encourage the children to work together to construct a model of a traffic light system for a road intersection. Explain that they will need to connect the lights to the outputs of the buffer box. They will also need at least two sets of lights which need to switch on and off in a sequence. Show them how to try out various sequences to see if they would be safe. Let them experiment with different periods of time between the lights changing. Ask them to make one set of lights for a main road and another for a minor road. Explain that they should switch inputs on and off with various wait commands to keep green and red lights switched on for reasonable periods of time.

Follow-up
Ask the children to design a junction with a right-only filter system. Ask them to incorporate a pedestrian button into the lights: most busy junctions have a pedestrian system incorporated in them.

A level crossing

Age range
Nine to eleven.

Group size
Six to eight children.

What you need
Computer equipment with a buffer box, a control software package, switches (press or tilt switches),

equipment to make a gate (such as LEGO or woodworking equipment), bulbs, wiring, electric motors.

Starting points

If you have a level crossing near by, take the children to observe from a safe distance how it works. If not, use a diagram or reference book to explain. Discuss with the children how we keep cars from crossing the line when a train approaches. Explain that a gate is needed to keep cars off the line when a train approaches and/or a set of lights to control the traffic. The gates could be automatically operated by an approaching train or could be operated from a remote signal box. The set of lights needs to be automatically operated.

What to do

Ask each group of children to devise a level crossing with the help of the computer. Explain that the buffer box will need to have outputs to motors to raise and lower (or open and close) the gates. Remind the children that each motor requires two connections. Explain that the gate can be controlled by switches, one on the floor which switches off the motor when the gate touches it (that is, when the gate is shut) and the other a tilt switch which stops the motor when the gate is fully open. The gate could be activated by a hand switch from an operator or by an automatic device. Suggest that they could use a pressure pad placed under the line or path of the train. Ask the children initially to experiment with hand-held models. When they have checked out their system, suggest that they incorporate it into a model railway, if you have one.

Follow-up

Ask the children to experiment with lights and no gates to see which is the most efficient system. Which is easier to construct? Which should be safer?

An automatic lighting system

Age range

Nine to eleven.

Group size

Four to six children.

What you need

A computer system with a buffer box, a control software package, a light-sensitive switch, bulbs, wiring, LEGO or craft materials.

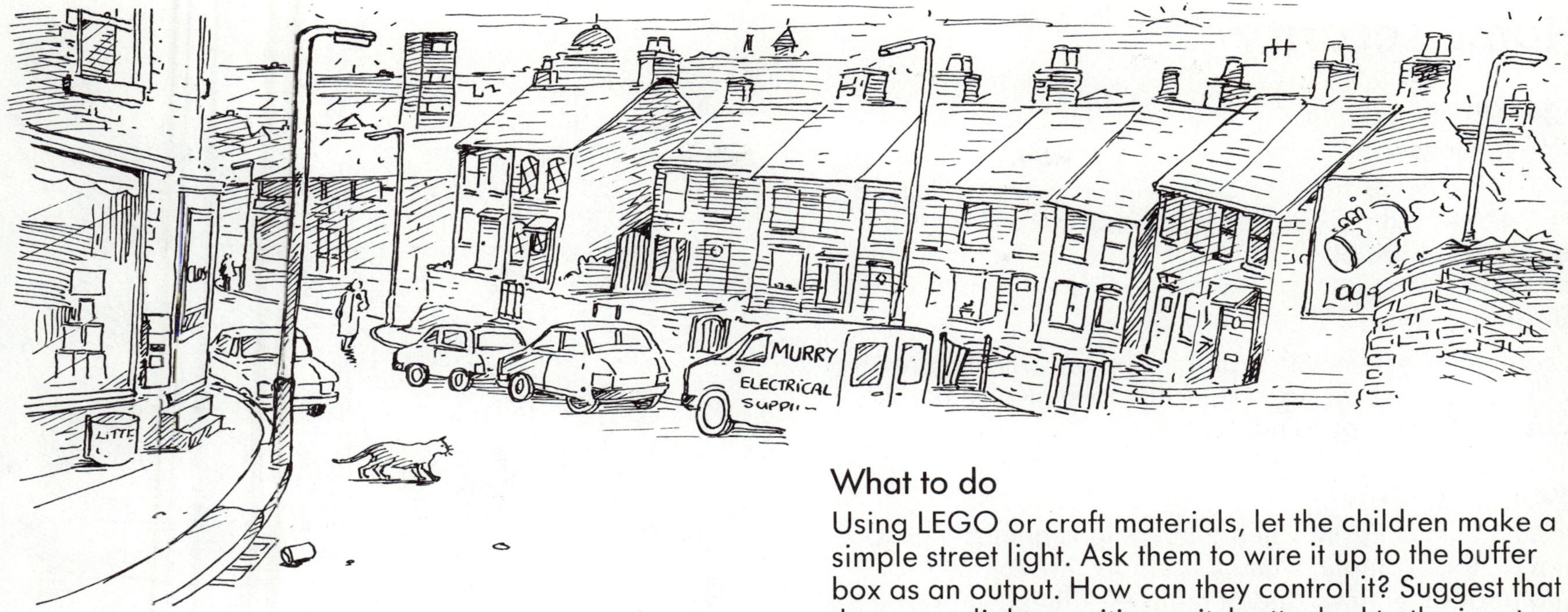

Starting points

Discuss with the children how street lights switch on and off. Does this happen at the same time each day or does it vary? Use newspapers to show the children the variation in lighting-up times. Alternatively, ask the children to note the times that street lights switch on outside their house, perhaps once a week for half a term. They will soon realise that the lights are activated by an automatic timing device. Explain that there are switches which are activated by light; they switch on or off depending on how much light they receive. Equally, the children could activate the lights on a time cycle worked out in advance. (Time cycle refers to the number of times the lights switch on and off.)

What to do

Using LEGO or craft materials, let the children make a simple street light. Ask them to wire it up to the buffer box as an output. How can they control it? Suggest that they use a light-sensitive switch attached to the inputs on the buffer box. For example, if the switch were attached to input 1 and if there were plenty of light reaching the switch, the lights should stay off. If the light to the switch is cut off, then the light will come on (if INPUT 1 on then SWITCH ON OUTPUT 1).

Ask the children if this is the best way of operating the light. Could they use a time device? This could be quite simple, for instance, SWITCH ON 1, WAIT, SWITCH OFF 1, WAIT . . .

The number following WAIT will decide how long the lights stay on or off.

Follow-up

Let the children attach a series of street lights to the buffer box. Invite them to incorporate them into a larger model which could include some traffic lights as well.

Home security

Age range

Nine to eleven.

Group size

Four to six children.

What you need

A computer system with a buffer box, a control software package, bulbs, wiring, a selection of switches, a doll's house or a cardboard model house.

Starting points

Discuss with children when a building is at most risk to thieves, for example, when it is empty, especially for long periods of time, and at night. Ask them what types of anti-theft measures can be taken. A burglar alarm is useful but suggest that another way is to persuade the would-be thieves that the house is occupied. Some lights could be left on but when a light is on continually, it is fairly obvious that the house is empty.

What to do

Suggest that the children design a device to switch on lights in sequence to make it appear that someone is at home. Ask the children to put bulbs in different rooms of the doll's or model house. Invite them to attach the bulbs to different outputs on the buffer box. Explain that they will need to tell the lights to switch on and off:
SWITCH ON 1, WAIT 5, SWITCH OFF 1, SWITCH ON 2, WAIT 25 . . .

Remind the children that they may require more than one light on at one time, that some lights, such as those

in the hall and landing, will tend to turn on for shorter periods of time, whereas the lounge light should stay on for longer periods. Point out that eventually the downstairs lights should be put out, the upstairs lights be switched on and then all the lights should go off.

Follow-up

- Suggest to the children that they install a light switch into their model which will start the whole sequence automatically when the switch senses that it is dark.
- Let the children investigate a selection of simple burglar alarms, warning lights and buzzers which are operated by switches or pressure pads.

Automatic doors

Age range
Nine to eleven.

Group size
Four to six children.

What you need
A computer system with a buffer box, a control software package, electric motors, switches (pressure-pad, press or magnetic switches), wiring, a small winch or pulley, materials to make model sliding, up-and-over or conventional doors (such as LEGO or woodwork materials).

Starting points
Discuss with the children the various kinds of automatic doors that they will have seen at the supermarket, at the shopping mall entrance or in the lift in the local department store or multi-storey car park. Point out that the doors not only need a mechanism for opening and shutting but also a method of keeping the doors open while people walk through.

What to do
Explain to the children that you want them to devise an automatic door system. Point out that they will first need to build a set of doors and an opening mechanism. Sliding doors will need runners; conventional doors will need hinges. LEGO sets will provide most of the items needed but the children could easily make doors from light wood struts and thick card. Give the children a pair of electric motors to open and shut the doors, and a

winch or pulley mechanism. Ask them to decide what to use to operate the doors – a pressure pad to open the doors when someone steps on it or a press switch. Remind them that the motors will need two connections from the output sockets. Explain that they will also need to build in a time delay. Tell them to work out how long to allow after the switch has been activated before the door shuts. Explain that the switch should be connected to an input socket so it could be programmed:

IF INPUT 1 ON then OUTPUT 1 and 2 on. WAIT 10.
OUTPUT 3 and 4 ON.

In this case, the pressure pad is pressed, one motor drags the doors open, the program waits for a pre-set time and then the other motor drags the doors shut. If the switch is activated during the 'Wait' sequence, the door will stay open; it will only shut when it receives no further 'Open' command. Point out to the children that this simulates the action of supermarket doors reacting to a flow of people.

Follow-up

Ask the children to design up-and-over doors for a garage and to combine the door opening with a light mechanism.

Lifts – going up!

Age range

Nine to eleven.

Group size

Four to six children.

What you need

A computer system with a buffer box, a control software package, materials for constructing a lift (such as LEGO or craft materials), electric motors, press or magnetic switches.

Starting points

Discuss with the children how lifts work. To start with, concentrate on a lift which travels from a ground floor to a first floor. How does the lift stop at the end of its travel? What moves the lift up and down? What does the lift run up and down in?

What to do

Ask the children to construct a lift and lift shaft using LEGO or craft materials. Suggest that they control it with a magnetic switch as a magnet on the lift could make contact with the magnet on the switch to stop the lift moving at a given point. Alternatively, press switches at the top and bottom would work well too. Point out that they will need two other press switches to activate the lift (to replicate the floor selection buttons found inside a real lift). Explain that they will need to winch the lift up the shaft and another motor to lower the lift back down again.

After the children have made the model, ask them to program the software to start the lift moving up or down when a switch is pressed. The lift should stop when it makes contact with a switch at the top or bottom of the shaft. It should then wait until it is operated up or down again.

Follow-up

Ask the children to design a lift with automatic doors which will move on several floors and can be called from any floor.

Sensing your surroundings

A computer can be linked to an array of sensors and, with suitable software, can be used to capture information from its surrounding environment. For example, you could connect your computer to sensors which record the air temperature and leave the system to record the variations in temperature over a set period of time. The computer will record that data and display it quickly and neatly so that you can analyse it. This process is referred to as data logging or data capture. It is quite distinct from work concerning databases because it is concerned with the capture of 'raw' data as it is produced. This type of work is probably best attempted with years five and six.

To carry out data logging, you will need a collection of sensors. The most common type is one that records temperature but there are others which will react to sound, light and almost any other environmental factor. It is easy to connect up sensors on some computers as the ports required are already installed in the machine. Some machines, however, will need extra ports fitted before you can make the necessary connections.

You will also need a software package to manage the whole process, collate the information and allow you to print off graphs of results. There are several of these packages available for different computers. For advice on sensors, connections and data logging packages, it is worth contacting your local advisory service for IT or Science and Technology.

It is possible to buy small weather stations which you can plug into your computer system to log over a period of time the maximum and minimum air temperatures, wind speed and direction and so on. These systems include software dedicated to its specialist purpose and can prove relatively inexpensive and easy to install.

Measuring room temperature

Age range

Nine to eleven.

Group size

Four to six children.

What you need

A computer system, a temperature sensor, a data-logging software package, a printer.

Starting points

It is probably best to attempt this activity at a time when the school's heating system is in use. Talk to the children about how temperature inside the classroom varies over time. Is it warmer in the afternoon than the morning? Is Monday morning as warm as other days in the week? Is the classroom exposed to the sunlight and what times of day will it affect the temperature in the classroom? Ask them what will happen to the temperature of the classroom overnight. When is the heating switched on and off?

What to do

Tell the children that they are to record the temperature of the classroom with the help of the computer. Choose two days of the week (one should preferably be Monday when the heating is recovering from the weekend lay-off). Show the children how to set up the computer, sensors and software and how to set the program to log temperatures from as early in the morning as possible. Encourage the children to note the time they start and ensure that they stop the process at the same time the next day.

Ask the children to watch the weather report on television and to make a note of the daytime and night-time temperatures for their area (the local television news will probably be best for this). Alternatively, most local newspapers and the broadsheet nationals give accurate maximum and minimum temperatures for most areas of Britain. Suggest that the children also record when sunshine (if any) played a part in warming the room. Were any of the windows open at any time?

At the end of the experiment, ask the children to save the results. Most software packages will allow you to make graphs of the data. For this example, a line graph will be most helpful as it will show the children how temperatures vary over a period of time.

The graphs should provide a wealth of information on which to base theories. Can the children plot when the heating came on or began to affect temperature? Did the temperature rise uniformly? Did the temperature reach a plateau and even off or did it continue to rise throughout the day? When did the heating system switch off? How did the room lose temperature? Did the temperature fall quickly or slowly throughout the night? Ask the children to add information on outside temperatures to their graph, also any data on the

amount and timing of sunlight, when windows were opened and so on.

Encourage the children to draw conclusions on the insulation of the room. How rapid was the loss of temperature at night? Is the heating system adequately controlled? Did the temperature of the classroom continue to rise above comfortable levels (18–20°)? If this did happen, are there individual thermostats fitted? Are they working properly or set too high?

Follow-up

Run a similar exercise but this time, ask the children to measure the temperature outside the classroom. The sensor is usually attached to the computer by a slim wire and it should be possible to give it access to the outside air without compromising classroom security (an airbrick is an ideal route). If you have two computer systems available, you could ask the children to record temperatures inside and outside the school over the same period of time.

How important is insulation?

Age range

Nine to eleven.

Group size

Four to eight children.

What you need

A computer system, a temperature sensor, a data-logging software package, a printer, a glass jar, insulating materials, hot water.

Starting points

Talk to the children about insulation. What clothes do we wear in winter? What materials make the warmest coats? How are homes insulated? Ask the children to find out what sort of insulation their home has, for example, roof insulation, double glazing, hot-water cylinder jackets, draught proofing, wall insulation and so on. Make a list of the possible types of insulation and ask them to tick off the types they have at home. Explain the importance of insulation – if you can cut down on the amount of heat escaping, you will not need to burn as much fuel to heat up the building.

What to do

Tell the children that they are to investigate how useful insulation can be. With the children's help, connect up the computer system and place the temperature sensor inside a large glass vessel. Pour in some very hot water and start the computer recording the water temperature for ten minutes. Ask the children to save the results and print off graphs. Invite the children to repeat the process but this time, let them insulate the glass jar in some way. Ask the children to compare the two sets of figures. How much has insulation slowed down the cooling process?

Follow-up

Let the children repeat the experiment with a range of insulating materials and discover which type of insulation is the most efficient.

How healthy is the fridge?

Age range

Nine to eleven.

Group size

Four to six children.

What you need

A computer system, a temperature sensor, a data-logging software package, a printer, a refrigerator.

Starting points

Talk to the children about the way a fridge keeps food fresh. What should the temperature inside a fridge be? What happens when the fridge door is opened? Is it important not to leave the door open unncessarily or to shut it as soon as possible when looking for food? How high or low should the fridge thermostat be set?

What to do

Explain to the children that they are to investigate the effect of a fridge door being opened. Set up the fridge and computer system next to each other. Arrange initially for the temperature sensor to be mounted on the middle shelf in the fridge. Allow the fridge to run until it reaches a low temperature (below 10°C). Ask the children to start the software recording the temperature. Let one of them open the door wide for one minute. Observe with the children from the screen display how far the temperature rises and how long it takes for the fridge to cool down again. Let the children repeat the procedure but explain that each time they should open the door for a longer period of time.

Follow-up

- Invite the children to repeat the experiment but this time ask them to open the door half-way. Let them try again, this time opening the door a quarter of its travel. Ask them to see how the distance they open the door affects heat gain inside the fridge.
- Let the children try the same experiment with a freezer in the school kitchens.
- Encourage the children to use the information they have collected to prepare a poster or leaflet, perhaps for parents, on energy-saving tips around the home.

Soil temperatures

Age range
Nine to eleven.

Group size
Four to six children.

What you need
A computer system, a temperature sensor, a data-logging software package, a printer, tubs filled with soil, a lamp which can hold a powerful (120W or more) reflector-type bulb.

Starting points
Talk to the children about how the sun heats up the ground and how this can affect temperatures. How quickly does soil heat up? How quickly might it cool down?

What to do
Tell the children that they are to collect information, with the computer's help, on the temperature of the soil. There are several ways they could do this. One would be to fill a large tub with earth and sink a temperature probe into the tub. Ask the children to put the tub into a dark area and set the software up to measure the soil temperature. Tell them to simulate the sun with the aid of an anglepoise lamp fitted with a powerful reflector bulb.

Alternatively, ask the children to place the tubs outside the classroom on a sunny day (some advance research into the weather forecast might be useful here). Encourage the children to plot the temperature of the

soil as it gains heat from the sun (or lamp) and also to log the decline in heat as the sun loses its power or when the lamp is turned off. Ask them to print off graphs and to save the data.

Follow-up

Let the children run a similar experiment on water temperatures. The two types of experiment could form the basis of a practical investigation into the distinction between maritime and continental climates. The children could compare the different ways in which soil and water gain and lose heat – water gains and loses heat more slowly. Ask them to compare temperature figures for the British climate with those of Central Europe and encourage them to explain why our country has generally cooler summers and milder winters than Central Europe.

Lighting-up times

Age range

Nine to eleven.

Group size

Four to six children.

What you need

A computer system, a temperature sensor, a data-logging software package, a printer, light sensors.

Starting points

Talk to the children about how the amount of light in a room changes. Is their classroom brighter when the sun shines or when the lights need to be used? Do the light levels vary with the seasons? Does the length of night vary with the seasons?

What to do

Explain to the children that they are to log light levels over quite a long period of time. They may need to spread the work over several terms and culminate it at the end of the school year. Let them choose one day each month and use the computer system and software to log the light levels over a 24 hour period. Ensure that the children save their work and print off graphs at the end of each session. Ask them to collate their graphs and observations in a folder.

Make sure that the children attach information on the outside weather conditions to each day's information. This should include the outside air temperature. Also, ask them to record the dates and times of the start and end of each recording session. In the summer term, let the children display all the material collected, together with any conclusions they may have drawn.

Follow-up

Select a room such as a store cupboard. If it has an electrical socket (to run your computer) and little outside light it will prove ideal. Let the children log the light levels in the room over a period of time and ask them to determine a pattern of how frequently the room is used. How often do people visit it? What time of day is most popular? How long do people tend to stay? Remember, the light sensor should react each time the room's light is switched on.

Making music

Increasingly, the classroom computer is being used for different and wider-ranging applications. The programme of study for Key Stage 1, Information Technology Capability, states that pupils 'should know that information can be held in a variety of forms, for example, words, numbers, pictures, sounds'.

Where the computer can be used to create sound, there is a wide range of different music software available, with packages to suit any computer. There are, however, certain extra peripherals you will need to generate sound or music.

Firstly, the computer must have a midi interface fitted or plugged into it. Some computers have this fitted as standard; for others it has to be bought and fitted internally. Other midi interfaces come in an external box which you can plug in or remove from the computer as and when you need to use it.

Secondly, there is a range of music software which, in order to utilize its full potential, should be used in conjunction with an electronic music keyboard. This must also have a midi interface fitted which can then be connected by leads to the midi interface at the computer.

Once you have the peripherals, it is time to look at the software. This can be grouped into two sections:

- Computer programs with pictures that represent sounds which can be organised to produce a sequence of sounds or tunes.
- Computer programs that display a musical stave on screen which can have musical notation placed on it to generate a tune before it is listened to.

This second type of program also varies in the facilities that are offered. Some programs allow the notes played on the music keyboard to be generated on the computer screen; others do not.

Most packages have in common the ability to play the finished composition through the musical keyboard, whatever method is used for linking sounds together at the computer. This means that the music can be played in the style of any of the musical instruments that the music keyboard can mimic.

Alternatively, the computer itself can be used to produce sound.

Some packages allow the music created to be recorded on to a cassette tape. To do this, you will need to connect a cassette recorder to your computer. While the computer plays the music created, switch the cassette recorder to record and the music can then be taped. This means that the music can be listened to away from the computer, thus leaving the computer available for the next group to use.

Most music software packages allow for a print-out to be produced, so you might need a printer. Programs that use pictures to represent sounds usually print out the pictures chosen and these can be displayed on classroom walls. Where the software uses a stave displayed on the screen, the score of music made can be printed out. This allows the music to be looked at away from the computer, while editing of the notes and further checking can be done on the computer at another time. This, of course, assumes that the music or sounds created have been saved to a computer disk. Ensure the children know how to do this and encourage them to save all their musical compositions for use at a later date.

Funny doorbells

Age range
Five to seven.

Group size
A small group.

What you need
A computer system, a music package that uses pictures to represent sounds, a printer, large sheets of painting paper, pencils, crayons, paints, scissors.

Starting points
Let the children imagine they are at home. Discuss with them how they know when someone is at the front door. Does their front door have a knocker or does it have a doorbell? What does the door knocker sound like? Ask them to make the sound. What does the doorbell sound like? Can they make the sound?

What to do

Explain to the children that they are going to make up their own doorbell 'music'. Load the music package. Let the children listen to the sounds of the pictures. Show them how to select and order the sounds they like to make a tune for their own doorbell. Show them how to save the tune so that they can play it again.

Demonstrate how to print out the pictures that make up their doorbell tune. Ask them to make a picture of a doorbell to display with the tune.

Follow-up

- Ask the children to make a repeating doorbell tune.
- Let them make a series of different doorbell tunes for a street of houses.
- Ask them to make a special doorbell tune for the school's front door.

Advertising jingle

Age range

Seven to nine.

Group size

Small groups.

What you need

A computer system, a music package that uses pictures to represent sounds, a printer, a cassette recorder, a cassette tape, paper, pencils.

Starting points

Discuss with the children the idea of packaging and marketing a particular product they have developed such as a new type of chocolate bar. Talk with them about the advertisements they see on the television or hear on local radio stations. Many of the advertisements have jingles where words about the products are set to music.

What to do

Together, work out the words for a jingle to advertise a chocolate bar. Suggest that the children type the words into a word processor and use them later for display.

Load the music package into the computer. Let the children listen to the sounds of the pictures. Show them how to select and order the sounds that will fit with the words of the jingle they made earlier. Let the children play the jingle music and ask them to sing the words to it.

Show the children how to save the jingle music so that they can play it again later. Let them print out the pictures of the sounds used for the jingle and display them on the classroom wall, along with a print-out of the words. Ask the children to design and make the packaging for the chocolate bar and incorporate these into the display.

Follow-up

- It is possible to connect a cassette recorder to the computer. When the children play their jingle, record it on to a cassette tape. This will allow them to listen to it and sing along away from the computer. Ask the children to record different tunes for the same words so that everyone can share each other's tunes.
- Using only the print-outs, let groups of children sing the tunes created by other children.

Musical acting

Age range

Five to seven.

Group size

The whole class.

What you need

A computer system, a music package that uses pictures to represent sounds.

Starting points

Ask the children how they usually receive instructions. It is usually when someone speaks to them. Ask them to consider what alternative means of communication could be used, for example, different types of music.

What to do

Discuss with the children the idea of being very still and of only being active when they hear a particular tune that has been assigned to them. Ask them to pretend that this is the music that brings them to life. It could be a happy, bouncy tune or a sad, plodding one.

Load the music package into the computer. Play the sounds of the pictures to the children. Divide the children into groups of three or four. Assign each group a particular picture and make sure they know how to act when their picture or tune is played by the computer.

Explain that they may have to perform bouncy, happy actions or slow, plodding ones, depending on the mood of their particular sounds. Create a long tune from the pictures and play it to the children. Ask them to listen to it carefully and make sure they know when their sound is used in the tune; is it near to the start or the end of the tune, or does it come somewhere in the middle? Ensure that they know when to be active and how to move. How long each group is active or still depends on the composition of the whole tune.

Follow-up

- Let a group of children create a long tune from the computer program and allocate each picture in the tune to another group of children who know when to come to life and when to be still.
- Choose a set of happy pictures from the program and ask a group of children to act them out. Then choose a set of sad pictures. Ask the other children how the movements of the active children have changed.

Mood music

Age range
Nine to eleven.

Group size
Small groups.

What you need
A computer system, a music package that uses pictures to represent sounds, a cassette recorder, a cassette tape.

Starting points
Ask the children how they could make their class presentation different by using 'computer-generated music'.

What to do
Discuss a presentation that the class is planning. It could be an assembly or a production for parents. Talk with the children about generating some background music for the presentation.

Load the music package. Show the children how to change the pictures and sounds available to them. Let them choose the tune file appropriate to the mood of music they require. For example, the tune file could represent a foreign country such as China or Egypt. Show the children how to listen to the sounds and how to select and order them to produce a longer tune.

Let the children order the pictures and their associated sounds to create the mood music. Show them how to save the tune so that they can use it later for the presentation. Show the children how to change or edit the tune to enhance it.

Follow-up

- Connect the cassette recorder to the computer and, while the tune is being played by the computer, ask the children to record it on to the cassette tape.
- Let small groups of children make their own mood music to play to the rest of the class, one group at a time. Discuss with the class what sort of mood the groups created with the music.
- Away from the computer, ask the children to prepare other resources needed for the presentation such as text for speech or pictures for visual aids.

Funny car horns

Age range

Eight to eleven.

Group size

Pairs.

What you need

A computer system, a music package that generates a stave of music on the screen and allows notes to be put on the stave from a music keyboard, a printer, a music keyboard, large sheets of drawing paper, pencils, crayons, paints, scissors.

Starting points

As part of a transport topic, discuss with the children what car horns sound like and when drivers use their car horns.

What to do

Make sure the music keyboard is connected to the computer through the midi interface and load the music software. Ensure that the software is set up to receive the inputs from the music keyboard. Explain to the children that they are going to try to make some car horn sounds on the music keyboard. It can be as creative or funny as they wish.

Let the children experiment on the music keyboard, making their own car horn sounds. The notes they play will appear on the computer screen. Show the children how to reset the software to make it ready to receive other car horn sounds. Once the children have created a satisfactory car horn sound, show them how to save it so that they can listen to it another day. Let them print out the music score that they have created. Away from the computer, ask the other children to design and create vehicles which will use the car horn sounds.

Follow-up

- Using this type of music package, ask the children to develop a musical jingle to accompany words that they have prepared and written in advance.
- Let the children use the package to generate mood music for a presentation they are to give.
- Give the children copies of the printed-out music score to create the car horn sounds on other instruments.

Instruments of the orchestra

Age range

Nine to eleven.

Group size

The whole class to begin with, then small groups at the computer.

What you need

A computer system, a music package that allows notes to be put on a stave from the computer keyboard and displayed on the screen, a printer, a musical keyboard, paper and pencils.

Starting points

Let the children listen to *Peter and the Wolf*. Discuss with them how the characters in the story are represented by musical themes, each played by different instruments of the orchestra. Talk about the families of instruments within the orchestra – woodwind, brass, strings and percussion, and the instruments within those families.

What to do

Divide the children into small groups and let each group write a story with a central character who is a musical instrument. Ask the children to give the character a name, for example, Vicki Violin. When the children have written their story, ask them to compose a tune, using the computer, for the story's character.

Make sure the music keyboard is connected to the computer through the midi interface so that the music is played through the music keyboard. Show the children how to load the music software. Show them how to put notes on to the stave on the screen using the computer keyboard.

Before they play the tune, show the children how to make sure that the music keyboard is set up to sound like the instrument the character represents, for example, a violin for Vicki Violin. In this way, the tune will sound as if it is being played by a violin.

Show the children how to save their music to disk to play another time. Let them print out the music so that they can play it on any instrument not connected to the computer.

Follow-up

- Let the groups collaborate to produce a story which includes many characters and will therefore have many associated tunes.
- Ask the children to tell their stories and play their tunes to other groups within their class or to groups of children from other classes in the school. Suggest that one group stays at the computer and plays the tune for each character as it is mentioned in the story.

Poetry music

Age range

Eight to eleven.

Group size

Small groups.

What you need

A computer system, a music package that allows notes to be put on a stave from the computer keyboard and displayed on the screen, a printer, a musical keyboard, paper, pencils.

Starting points

Let the children listen to a poem that is read to music or has been set to music.

What to do

Discuss with the children the idea of setting the scene with music for a piece of poetry that they could write. Talk about the possible mood of the poem. Is it happy or sad, scary or fast or slow? Point out to the children that the mood of the poetry should be reflected in the mood of the music.

Make sure the music keyboard is connected to the computer by the midi interface so that the music is played through the music keyboard. Load the music software. Show the children how to put notes onto the stave on the screen.

Ask the children to write their poetry in groups. Let those who have completed their poem work at the computer to create the music to accompany it. Show the children how to save on disc their poem music to play for the rest of the class on another day. Let the children print out the score of their music.

Follow-up

Let the children use the print-out of their music score to play the accompaniment on another musical instrument.

Resources

Suggested reading

One of the best sources of information and ideas for teaching computer activities in the primary classroom is MAPE (Micros and Primary Education – see below for address and telephone number). Membership entitles you to a free subscription to their quarterly magazine *Micro-Scope*, as well as numerous curriculum 'specials'. You might also like to read some of the following books.

Children Using Computers, A. Straker (1989) Basil Blackwell

Computers and Learning: Helping Children Acquire Thinking Skills, D. M. Underwood and G. Underwood (1990) Basil Blackwell

Computers and the Primary Curriculum 3-13, R. Crompton (1989) The Falmer Press

Information Technology from 5 to 16 (Curriculum Matters 15), Department of Education (1989) HMSO

I.T. in the National Curriculum, I. Birnbaum (1990) RESOURCE

Micros for Children with Special Needs, M. H. Hope (1987) Souvenir Press

Non-statutory Guidance for Teachers: Information Technology in the National Curriculum, Curriculum Council for Wales (1990) HMSO

Non-statutory Guidance: Information Technology Capability, National Curriculum Council (1991) HMSO

Technology in the National Curriculum, Department of Education (1990) HMSO

Suppliers of computer resources

4Mation, 14 Castle Park Road, Whidden Valley, Barnstaple, Devon EX32 8PA. Tel. 0271 25353. Producers of software for BBC and Archimedes computers.

Acorn Computers Ltd, Cambridge Techno Park, 645 Newmarket Road, Cambridge CB5 8PD. Tel. 0223 245200.

Beebug, 117 Hatfield Road, St Albans, Herts AL1 4JS. Tel. 0727 40303. Suppliers of hardware and software for Acorn machines.

Brilliant Computing, PO Box 142, Bradford BD9 5NF. Tel. 0274 497617. Suppliers of peripherals and software for special needs.

Computer Concepts, Gadesden Place, Hemel Hempstead, Herts HP2 6EX. Tel. 0442 63933. Suppliers of software.

The Concept Keyboard Co., Moorside Road, Winnall Industrial Estate, Winchester, Hampshire SO23 7RX. Tel. 0962 843322. Suppliers of concept keyboards.

Deltatronics, Church Road Industrial Estate, Gorslas, Llanelli SA14 7NF. Tel. 0269 843728. Suppliers of computer control hardware.

ESM Ltd, Duke Street, Wisbech, Cambs PE13 2AE. Tel. 0945 63444. Suppliers of a range of primary software.

Fernleaf Educational Software, Fernleaf House, 31 Old Road West, Gravesend, Kent DA11 0LH. Tel. 0474 359037. Suppliers of software for Acorn computers and distributors of Pip programmable robot.

Hybrid, 88 Butt Lane, Cambridge CB4 6DG. Tel. 0223 861522. Suppliers of peripherals, especially for special needs and music.

Jessop Ralph Ltd, Unit 5, 7 Long Street, London EC2 8HN. Distributors of the Jessop Turtle.

LEGO UK Ltd, Educational Department, Ruthin Road, Wrexham, Clwyd LL13 7TQ. Tel. 0978 290900. Suppliers of LEGO control resources.

Lindis UK, Wood Farm, Linstead Magna, Halesworth, Suffolk IP19 0DU. Tel. 098 685 476. Suppliers of peripherals, most notably the Touch Window.

Longman-Logotron Ltd, 124 Cambridge Science Park, Milton Road, Cambridge CB4 4ZS. Tel. 0223 425558. Suppliers of a range of software for Acorn computers, including LOGO.

MAPE (Micros and Primary Education), Roger Keeling, Newman Software, Newman College, Genners Lane, Bartley Green, Birmingham BT32 7EZ. Tel. 021 476 1181. An organization which promotes the use of IT in primary education.

Microvitec plc, Futures Way, Bolling Road, Bradford, West Yorks BD4 7TU. Tel. 0274 390011. Suppliers of monitors, touch screens, etc.

MUSE, PO Box 43, Houghton on the Hill, Leicester LE7 9GX. Tel. 0533 433839. Suppliers of Nimbus software.

NCET (National Council for Educational Technology), Sir William Lyons Road, University of Warwick Science Park, Coventry CV4 7EZ. Tel. 0203 416994. A registered charity funded by the government, promoting and developing the use of educational technology in every field of education and training.

Newman Software, Newman College, Genners Lane, Bartley Green, Birmingham B32 3NT. Tel. 021 476 1181. Suppliers of software for Nimbus and Acorn computers.

Research Machines Ltd, Mill Street, Oxford OX2 0BW. Tel. 0865 791234. Suppliers of Nimbus computers.

Northwest SEMERC, Fitton Hill CDC, Rosary Road, Oldham OL8 2QE. Tel. 061 627 4469. Suppliers of educational software.

RESOURCE, Exeter Road, Doncaster DN2 4PY. Tel. 0302 340331. Suppliers of educational software and publications.

Sherston Software, Swan Barton, Sherston, Malmesbury, Wilts SN16 0LH. Tel. 0666 840433. Suppliers of educational software.

Valiant Technology Ltd, Myrtle House, 69 Salcott Road, London SW11 6DQ. Tel. 071 924 2366. Suppliers of the Valiant Turtle and Roamer.